Entertaining for Business

Entertaining

for

Business

A Complete Guide to Creating Special Events
with Style and a Personal Touch

NANCY KAHAN

WITH ELEANOR BERMAN

PHOTOGRAPHS BY MICHAEL SKOTT

DESIGNED BY DON MORRIS WITH RICHARD FERRETTI

CLARKSON N. POTTER, INC./PUBLISHERS

To the memory of my mother and grandmother, who encouraged me to pursue a career and who were always the life of the party.

And to my son, Billy, whose sense of humor and smiling face have been a constant source of joy in my life.

N.K.

Photographs on pages 21, 63, 178, and 179 by Steve Adams. Bottom photograph on page 48 and photographs on pages 49–51 by Mariette Pathy Allen for Karin Bacon Events, Inc. Photographs on page 176 by Susan Magrino.

Text copyright © 1990 by Nancy Kahan and Eleanor Berman.
Photographs copyright © 1990 by Michael Skott.

Published by Clarkson N. Potter, Inc., and distributed by Crown Publishers, Inc., 201 East 50th Street, New York, New York 10022

CLARKSON N. POTTER, POTTER, and colophon are trademarks of Clarkson N. Potter, Inc.

Manufactured in Japan

Library of Congress Cataloging-in-Publication Data

Kahan, Nancy.
    Entertaining for business : A complete guide to creating special events with style and a personal touch / Nancy Kahan with Eleanor Berman ; photographs by Michael Skott.
        p.   cm.
    1. Business etiquette.   2. Business entertaining.   3. Public relations.   I. Berman, Eleanor, 1934–   .   II. Title.
HF5389.K35   1990
395'.3—dc19   89-3849

ISBN 0-517-57080-7
10 9 8 7 6 5 4 3 2 1

First Edition

Acknowledgments

To Michael Skott, our friend and inspired photographer, who traveled far and wide to shoot the "perfect party." We couldn't have done it without his patience, his spirit, and his discerning eye; to Carol Southern for her confidence that we could do it; to Nat Wartels, Alan Mirken, and Bruce Harris, who said yes; to Don Morris and Richard Ferretti, who captured our philosophy of business entertaining in the design of this book; to Pam Krauss, our editor, who was with us every step of the way and who knew what was necessary and what was not; to Gael Towey and Dania Martinez, who brought their special visions to this book; to Connie Clausen, whose enthusiasm was always with us; to Martha Schueneman for staying on top of so many details; to Cate Cummings, the calm in the eye of the storm; to Teresa Nicholas and Amy Boorstein, who painstakingly saw the book through every stage; to the professionals who shared their time and their knowledge so graciously; to the companies who allowed their parties to be photographed; to my publicity staff, who were vital to the success of so many of these parties; and a special thanks to Marie Garcia, who supported me on the home front. Thank you all.

Contents

Introduction

I'VE ALWAYS LOVED PARTIES. Growing up as the youngest of five in a gregarious and garrulous Irish family, I often found myself surrounded by family and friends, all singing, dancing, talking, and laughing. It was part of the fabric of our lives, and I always delighted in being a part of it. It's hardly surprising that I have continued this tradition in my own family and incorporated it into my business life as well.

When I went looking for my first job, full of enthusiasm but with little idea of how to direct it, the head of the employment agency I visited asked, "Have you ever thought of publicity? It would be perfect for you—you'll write press releases and give parties." Well, she was absolutely right. I did plenty of copywriting, and over the years I have planned and produced more than 300 parties—some intimate, some outrageous, some simple, some grand, and even a few disasters. I have learned from them all.

One of the most important things I've learned is that business entertaining is quite different from personal entertaining. If that were not the case, there really would be no need for this book; many wonderful books on entertaining have already been published and would certainly suffice. So you won't find any recipes for hors d'oeuvres or show-stopping desserts in this book—only detailed recipes for successfully planning and orchestrating a business party for groups of 20 or 2,000. The fact is that entertaining for business requires an enormous amount of advance planning, attention to detail, and imagination. You may not need to worry about how many shrimp to serve (the caterer will take care of that) or how many glasses you'll need, but you do need to know how to put your guests at ease and how to create an atmosphere of warmth. And these are not simple tasks. When entertaining family or friends at home, you have built-in intimacy and a comfortable atmosphere in which most, if not all, of your guests will know each other. At a business party, however, most of your guests will be strangers who will very often feel shy and a bit out of place. The space you are using may be cold and forbidding. And many of the guests will be there because their job requires them to be, not necessarily because they want to be there. These are tough obstacles to overcome, but they are surmountable.

When I've attended an event that doesn't work for one reason or another, I inevitably wonder how different it might have been if only the planners of the event had put themselves into the shoes of their guests, and put more thought into making people feel comfortable rather than trying to impress them. I wrote this book with the goal of helping people think of small, personal touches that change a party atmosphere from impersonal to intimate.

The parties we selected for inclusion in this book are all quite different, but they share one essential ingredient: warmth and an element of drama. We tried to include parties from as many different fields of business as possible, including finance, law, advertising, publishing, and the art world, and to show parties on different scales. Naturally, because my business has been book publishing, you will find a predominance of book parties. But while you may not have a built-in focal point in the form of a best-selling book to promote, the elements that made these parties successes can be applied to any area of business entertaining.

I wanted to share what I've learned (sometimes quite painfully) about the "art" of business entertaining. And while that may sound a bit pretentious, "art" is what it can be if it is done with imagination, attention to detail, and concern for the guests. I hope this book will inspire you. I hope it will help you focus on why you are giving the party, what you intend to get from it, and what elements are most necessary to making it happen. And I hope it will provide some practical solutions to the problems you will inevitably face if you are going to entertain for business. It is a challenging job but one that brings rewards on so many levels. And when done right, one that will bring both you and your guests great pleasure.—N.K.

Parties with a Purpose

BUSINESS ENTERTAINING is bigger today than ever before. Each year billions of dollars are spent on parties for clients, customers, employees, and the media—and for good reason. Well-planned entertaining is a sound investment. It is one of the most effective ways a company can communicate on a personal level with a large or small group of people, be they employees, clients, or potential clients.

Chapter

1

Entertaining reflects the company image in a direct way that no other medium can match. It can also demonstrate how innovative a company can be.

Yet despite all the money and manpower involved, companies often settle for events that are ordinary, even boring. Giving a humdrum, boring party is a waste of money—and, even more important, a wasted opportunity. I have seen the value of creative corporate entertaining proven over and over again. Many of these parties have played an important role in building enthusiasm for new products and creating goodwill both in and out of the company—simply because the guests enjoyed themselves and remembered their hosts with warmth.

In order for business entertaining to accomplish its full potential benefits, it should not be considered separately, but included as part of the company's overall marketing and public relations strategy. Each party should have carefully planned objectives, just as an advertising or public relations campaign would.

Don't underestimate the benefits parties can produce because they seem intangible. Goodwill sounds vague until you think of it in terms of a warmer reception for your salespeople. A company party is not just an obligation at Christmas but an opportunity to instill employee loyalty and inspire higher productivity.

In businesses such as mine, where publicity is an important aspect of promoting products, parties can play a key role in launching new ventures. Advertising, which costs more, would have far less impact. Opinion makers are much more likely to notice a feature story in the *New York Times* than a costly half-page advertisement appearing among many other similar ads in the same newspaper.

Above all, parties can be an important marketing tool, a way to position your company and its product. Our parties are intended to give booksellers the message that they can count on us to promote our books aggressively and with

Convention-al Wisdom

Conventions are the single most important opportunity for your company to attract new business, launch a new product, and position itself in the marketplace. Because the competition among companies for guests is inevitably fierce, many companies allocate the bulk of their entertainment budget to a single convention extravaganza.

Whether you plan a small or a grand event, there are some ground rules of convention entertaining you would do well to observe:

• Think twice before undertaking a "big" party at a convention. They are a major project and involve a great deal of time, effort, energy, and money. Despite all of that, they can be a highly effective way of making an impression for your company and your product.

• If you do decide to go for a gala event, do it right or not at all. The event will be making a statement about who your company and/or product is to a large market and you want it to be a strong, positive one. Also, allow plenty of time— at least six to nine months—for planning. And check out if there are other big parties scheduled to avoid conflicts.

• When the convention is out of town, consider hiring a professional party planner (see Chapter 4) who will secure locations and take care of all logistics involving caterers, florists, musicians, and lighting. It is well worth the expense since they can do the job of coordinating all of this from a distance best; something undoubtedly would fall between the cracks if you tried to do it all yourself.

• Do, however, take a "scouting trip" accompanied by the party planner you choose to check out several spaces, if possible six months in advance. If this is impossible, ask for photos, sketches, or video footage of the space. This is especially important if it is an unconventional space, such as a museum or a private home.

• The invitation must sell the event—make it unique, arresting, inviting. You will be competing with many other companies for the same guests at the same time. Be original. Be very

specific as to how many guests the invitation includes. Most people travel in pairs so be prepared for two guests for every acceptance. Give clear, easy-to-follow directions. Send them out at least one month before the event.

• I prefer having big parties later in the evening. Many clients have dinner commitments with other companies and this allows them to attend both functions in the same evening. I also think dancing is a great asset since people will be cooped up in a convention hall all day and hungry for some physical release.

• If it's a sit-down meal, insist on round tables and limit the number of guests at each to ten. Assign at least one staff person from the company to each table to act as host, introduce guests, and keep the flow of conversation going. Prep staff as to who the guests will be and what the goals of the event are. Rotate guests-of-honor between courses.

• At least a week in advance, assign staff their jobs and be specific as to who will check guests in at the door, introduce clients to company executives, give a welcome talk, give out favors (if appropriate). I think a receiving line is an excellent way of breaking the ice. Plan ahead for who will be standing where and how the line will be moved smoothly.

• Keep breakfasts and lunches short, simple, and as close to the convention hall as possible. Consider a deli-bag lunch in a nearby hotel space. It's fun, efficient, and economical. Save the wonderful out-of-the-way spaces for dinners or cocktail parties.

• Most people will be wearing their convention badges, but supply blank name tags for any nonconventioneers or unexpected guests.

• Because virtually all of your guests will be away from home and therefore without cars of their own, anticipate transportation needs. If your location is very out of the way, consider buses, trolleys, vans, or a private cab service. This is particularly important at the end of the evening in places cabs don't frequent.

style. It is a message any manufacturer would do well to send to its distributors, vendors, sales representatives—and competition.

By being more conscious of your entertaining goals, you may be able to plan parties with a bigger payoff. An anniversary party, for example, seems an obvious opportunity to point out that your organization has established itself successfully and is thriving. But with a little thought, the same event can accomplish even more.

When the House of Hermès, the home of the famous French designer scarves and accessories, marked its 150th birthday in 1987, all of Paris saw the party pavilion the company built on the Seine and the fireworks over the river that marked the date. Because the party was spectacular, the press coverage surpassed anything advertising might have bought. There were few people left in Paris who had not been reminded that Hermès is a local institution almost as old as the Eiffel Tower.

But the party's effect did not end that night. Hermès actually *marketed* its party decor, adorning much of its merchandise that season with a fireworks motif. The products helped remind an international audience of the anniversary and created curiosity that brought people into the stores, generating extra sales.

ADD UP THE PAYBACK

A PARTY, THEN, SHOULD BEGIN WITH a clear definition of its goals, both short and long term. That is the only way you can accurately determine how much it is worth to the company and can begin to assess what the budget should be.

Business Entertaining Goals

A well-thought-out party should be able to reach more than one valuable business objective with any given party. Here are some possibilities to consider:

- *developing rapport and understanding with customers and clients*
- *winning new clients or customers for your company*
- *communicating or enhancing the company image*
- *building awareness of the company in your market*
- *introducing new products*
- *announcing the opening of a new outlet*
- *improving employee morale and productivity*
- *attracting new employees*
- *celebrating a company anniversary or landmark*
- *creating goodwill within the community*
- *raising money for the benefit of a worthy cause*
- *generating publicity*

After you have considered all of the possible benefits, you are ready to determine specifically the following:

- why you are giving this party
- whom you are giving it for
- what you want to achieve
- what immediate results the company can hope to accomplish
- what long-term rewards are anticipated
- how much publicity can realistically be expected from the event.

Only when you have addressed these issues can you begin to consider your budget.

In an organization, the answers to these questions must not come only from the staff members charged with planning the party but should be shared by every department that is affected. Set up a meeting to discuss party goals with representatives from the departments involved. Remember to include the marketing director. In a small company, the president may even be invited.

A PARTY-PLANNING PHILOSOPHY

ONCE YOU'VE DECIDED WHAT YOU want to get out of the party, you figure out how best to focus your event—whether to go with a large-scale party or have a more intimate kind of affair. But whether it's large or small, never lose sight of your underlying goal. Business parties can serve diverse purposes, but the best of them begin with the same philosophy: focus on the guests, not your company. Instead of trying to impress them with the merits of your products or the services you offer, you should be trying to show them how much you appreciate and value them as clients or customers. And that takes more than money.

To do this you don't need an unlimited budget. You do it by refusing to settle for the ordinary, by using imagination and originality, injecting an element of warmth, surprise, and fun into the proceedings. Often, this means taking risks —not being afraid to try something new and different, to think big. The extra effort and imagination that go into creating an extraordinary party tells guests you think they are special—and sends them home feeling their host is quite special, too.

Being different doesn't mean looking for gimmicks, however. It is simply using the traditional elements of a party in a more creative way, seeking out innovative spaces and making more original use of backdrops, lighting, music, flowers, and food. These elements should not stand out individually, but fuse into an overall impression that wakes up the senses from the moment a guest enters the room.

Creating that kind of magic has much in common with mounting a successful theatrical event. Like that of a playwright, your goal is to come up with a scene that will involve and elate your audience. As the producer, you must work with budgets and contracts and hire the right professionals to handle many practical details, from microphones to coat checks. As the stage manager, you must remain in firm charge of your cast and crew, ensuring that each one shines in his role as part of the overall production. And as the director, you will set the tone for the entire event.

Secrets of a Great Party

- **PLAN AHEAD.** *Don't be overwhelmed by the decisions to be made. Start early and take things one step at a time.*
- **DON'T AIM TO IMPRESS, AIM TO DELIGHT.** *Think of surprising and pleasing people rather than impressing them.*
- **DON'T SETTLE FOR THE ORDINARY.** *Find a wonderful undiscovered space; select an unusual theme or menu. Don't be afraid to take risks.*
- **HIRE THE BEST PROFESSIONALS YOU CAN AFFORD.** *Talented pros make* you *look good.*
- **DON'T ASSUME ANYTHING.** *No matter how able the people you hire, remember that every cast needs a director. Remain responsible for seeing that no detail is forgotten.*
- **HAVE FUN!** *Remember that enjoyment is what parties are supposed to be all about.*

The All-Important Party File

A party file that is continually kept up to date is a must for anyone in charge of company parties and special events. The file should contain three separate sections:

● CHECKLISTS. *Lists like those found at the back of this book are insurance policies; using them guarantees that even the smallest elements of the party will be remembered. Adapt these lists to fit your own planning needs.*

● PAST PARTY RECORDS. *This file contains the names and addresses of suppliers and professionals who have performed well for your company parties, with their rates. It should be updated after each party. (Note suppliers who should* not *be used again as well.) The names are useful when you need sources in the future as well as when someone takes over the party-planning function after you.*

● FUTURE FILES. *This is another essential resource for finding talented professionals when you need them. When you hear about a creative party planner or caterer, write down the name immediately and put it into your future file. Watch also for magazine and newspaper articles about interesting parties and benefits and the people who created them. Clip items about people who perform special services, such as designing party invitations or providing unusual entertainment. Look for these stories when you travel as well as at home, since you never know when you may need help in a new city. Anything that has to do with entertaining belongs in this file—even write-ups of lavish weddings, because the people who design them may also be able to create something wonderful for other kinds of occasions more appropriate to your needs.*

A STEP-BY-STEP PLAN

NONE OF THIS IS DIFFICULT IF YOU approach party planning as a series of small steps, beginning well ahead of the actual party date to allow time for each essential detail. The chapters ahead will help you formulate your plan, starting with the first important step—setting realistic goals and budgets within the company. In the pages ahead you will also learn how to:

● choose the right caterers and party professionals
● read the fine print of a party contract
● find the right party space
● choose and execute a theme
● create a winning invitation
● plan interesting menus
● make the details count—from lighting and flowers to music
● ensure easy crowd flow
● make guests feel comfortable and involved in the festivities

● gain valuable media exposure and publicity for your event.

Above all, you will learn to personalize your parties and infuse them with warmth.

Finally, there will be a complete checklist to guide you through the process from the earliest planning stages right up to the day of the party, to make sure no detail is overlooked. That list should become part of what is an essential tool for a well-organized planner—a party file (see box above).

The suggestions and guidance in this book will be particularly helpful to those with little party-planning experience. Party professionals often find that the people charged with hiring them are very nervous about this responsibility. While some companies have staff hired especially to oversee entertaining, in the majority of offices there is no job description that specifically covers this function. An assistant to an executive, a member of the public affairs staff, or someone who simply inherits the job because there is no one else to do it may find himself or herself responsible for planning a major company event—with a major budget.

It isn't surprising, therefore, that these people sometimes feel overwhelmed by the task. Many have never entertained more than six or eight guests in their homes and have no idea where to begin when they are told to arrange an event for two to three hundred people. Panic and paralysis usually set in. They imagine that their jobs are on the line and the company's image is at stake. They worry because their bosses will be present at the affair and will expect everything to be letter perfect. They are afraid to take risks, so they tend to arrange predictable events that are conventional, safe, and totally without excitement.

If you find yourself in this position, the practical information offered in these pages should help you to approach your task with more assurance—and more style. But one of the most important lessons to keep in mind is that it is not necessary to obtain absolute perfection in order to have a successful party. Memorable entertaining begins and ends with the desire to make people happy. Noel Coward summed up one of the secrets to a great party when he said, "Good party givers have a talent to amuse."

Set out to create a party that *you* will enjoy, a party where *you* will have fun—and you can feel confident that your guests are going to enjoy themselves, too.

A Black-Tie Block Party

When the goal of a local organization is to raise money and a new office building needs to be introduced to the community, a joint event may accomplish both objectives.

That was the case when two unlikely neighbors in Houston joined forces. Heritage Plaza, the newest building in town, teamed up with the Heritage Society, an organization dedicated to preserving the city's oldest structures—which happen to stand in Sam Houston Park, right across the street from the skyscraper. The "block party" that resulted in the building lobby gave the society free space and an innovative theme for its annual dinner dance. And the event brought many prominent local citizens to admire the striking new building.

The new skyscraper looms behind the Heritage Society's oldest structure, *below*. Subtle lighting is an inexpensive way to warm up a cold space, *opposite*.

A Fresh Start in Manhattan

ON A FRESH spring morning in May, what nicer way to start the day than an elegant breakfast in Central Park Zoo, with New York's skyscrapers as a backdrop and the opportunity to visit magnificent zoo animals as a bonus? That was the treat planned by the New York Zoological Society to show off their newly refurbished facilities to their patrons, high-level donors to the New York Zoological Society.

WHO

NEW YORK
ZOOLOGICAL SOCIETY

WHAT

BREAKFAST

WHERE

CENTRAL PARK ZOO

WHY

TO HONOR NYZS
PATRONS

Patron support is as important to a nonprofit organization as are valued clients to a business, and this was a personal way for the Society to show appreciation to its supporters, as well as an opportunity to show off the zoo at its best. It also pointed up to the benefactors what a convivial party space the zoo is, in the interest of attracting further corporate business.

The Zoological Society decided on a breakfast for this occasion because it provides several advantages, explained Jill Alcott, the manager of special events for the Society. "We always find that we

A family of ducks, *above,* and the animated musical clock at the zoo's entrance, *right,* provided additional charm to the breakfast event. A "coffee hour" replaced the typical cocktail hour and allowed guests to mingle before settling down to eat, *opposite.*

get a good response to a breakfast," she says. "Our patrons are busy people with crowded schedules, but they seem to be able to find time to stop by on the way to work. Also, breakfast can be done nicely on a limited budget, something that is important to us. It requires less serving help and a less extensive menu. Using the zoo is a bonus; coming outdoors in the morning is a welcome way to start the day."

Breakfast events also reach people when they are fresh and most receptive, before they have been inundated with problems at the office. It was easy to see that these guests were relaxed and enjoying themselves as they stood around chatting over a first cup of coffee preceding the meal.

The zoo staff wanted the event to be elegant, but not formal or stuffy. They preferred a serve-

The unusual coolness of the May morning required the clear tent sides to be dropped down, *below,* but that did not obstruct the dramatic view of the city. A food and flower centerpiece, *opposite,* was both efficient and beautiful, and it blended well with the Zoological Society's stunning place settings.

yourself meal to allow for a flexible timetable, yet they did not want guests to have to stand in line at a buffet. They worked with Lavin's Caterers to devise a festive buffet basket for each table. Peter Thopiou of York Floral Company used his artistry to decorate the baskets that doubled as attractive centerpieces.

The zoo staff worked with the caterer and Broadway Famous Party Rentals to choose tablecloths and napkins, glassware, and silver urns and trays that would make the tables outstanding, adding the Zoological Society's own handsome china. Hand-lettered menus completed the elegant setting.

To ensure a successful party rain or shine, Stamford Tent and Equipment Company helped the planners devise a "crystal tent" with transparent sides that would serve to keep guests warm and dry

and still allow for spectacular views.

The events were planned to allow guests to spend as little or as much time at the party as their schedules allowed. The group was thanked personally and given an update on zoo news by the director. Following breakfast, many stayed to take advantage of personalized insiders' tours with zoo staff members. The final highlight for those who remained until 9:30 A.M. was the chance to watch a special sea lion behavioral demonstration.

The combination of greenery, wildlife, and the New York City skyline was a sure crowd pleaser, and using the park allows for a breath of country in the middle of Manhattan. Park and zoo outings are popular breaks in the business day in any town. The bigger the city, the more welcome the chance to be outdoors.

NEW YORK
ZOOLOGICAL
SOCIETY · 1895™

Following breakfast, guests had a special opportunity to observe trainers feeding the seals, *above,* as well as the tropical birds in the rain forest, *right.* These are attractions that delight guests of all ages. Richard Lattis, the zoo's director, and several staff members led individual tours, *opposite,* sharing fascinating information about the newly installed flora and fauna.

Patron Breakfast Menu
BY LAVIN CATERERS

Breakfast pastries: miniature croissants, Danish pastries, oat bran muffins, and banana nut bread

Fresh berries, pineapple, melons, strawberries, and grapes

Salad of marinated mandarin oranges in a Grand Marnier and fresh mint sauce

Figs with a California Pinot Noir, cinnamon, and basil sauce

Savory Onion Tart

Smoked Norwegian salmon rolls with spring vegetables

Chestnut Honey Butter, Lingonberry Preserves, Wild Thyme Butter, Huckleberry Puree, Unsalted New York State Butter

*Freshly Squeezed Orange Juice and Pink Grapefruit Juice
Brewed Coffee
Water-Decaffeinated Coffee
Assorted Teas*

Setting Party Budgets

FOR SOME COMPANIES the most important consideration of any business party is how much it will cost. This can be very shortsighted. If entertaining is a very small item in your firm's overall budget, it may be up to you to convince top management that spending more money on entertaining and doing your parties up right is more than worth the investment. Don't be afraid to ask for your share of the corporate pie.

Chapter

2

Cutting costs to keep a lean budget may mean the difference between an event that makes a statement and one that is a waste of everyone's time—and the company's money. Remember all the diverse goals that can be accomplished with business entertaining. A half-page advertisement in a national magazine such as *People* can cost as much as $30,000, an amount more than adequate for creating a newsworthy event that may attract local or even national TV and press coverage worth many times more than your investment.

The specific budget allocated for each party depends on what the firm stands to gain from it. If you can foresee TV or major print exposure, a party is certainly worth the cost of at least one major advertisement. The amount allotted should be generous in any case, reflecting the benefits of a long-

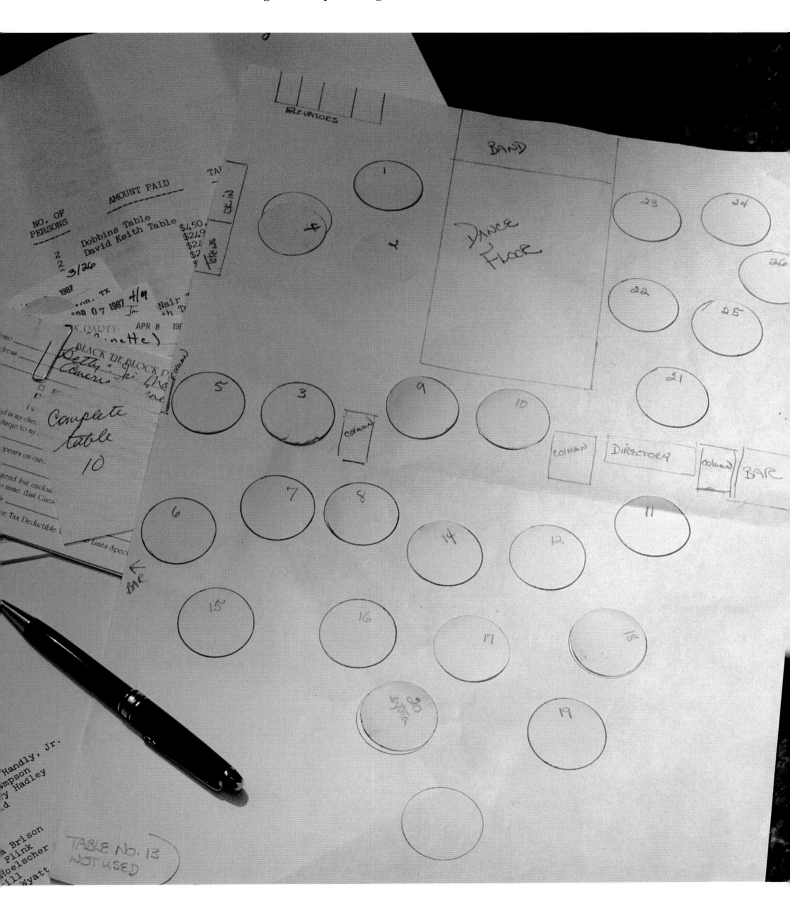

term investment. In many cases it makes sense to devote a percentage of projected sales to entertaining, just as you would for advertising or publicity.

THE BUDGET FOR INDIVIDUAL PARTIES depends in part on the size of your guest list. This will vary according to each party's goals. There are times when your best strategy is to invite as many people as you can—if you are launching a best-seller or a mass-market product, for example. But this is not always the case.

● **WHEN TO STAY SMALL.** When you want to reach a select, influential group or establish an exclusive image, a small party is your best choice—particularly if the invitation makes it clear that only a select group has been invited. (See Chapter 6 for wording of invitations.) Including guests often makes them feel more special in a small intimate group than they would as part of a mob scene. Limiting your gathering is often the only way to tempt top executives to accept your invitation. Neither the *House Beautiful* party on page 94 nor the Givenchy product introduction on page 180 would have reached its goal as effectively with a large event.

In my own company, when superstar Bette Midler wrote a whimsical autobiography called *The Life and Times of Baby Divine,* we deliberately scheduled a private and very personal party to launch the book. With such a visible personality, no party was necessary to attract media coverage. Instead, my goal was to create a comfortable rapport between the author and the people she was working with in the

company. Only a few key media contacts were included.

I borrowed a friend's Manhattan loft and had the caterer work out a menu of foods Bette particularly likes, especially her favorite, Middle Eastern cuisine. We also hired a disc jockey to play Bette's favorite records. This small, inexpensive gathering accomplished its goal of cementing good relations between Miss Midler and the staff. As an unexpected bonus, because the party was so special and so intimate, a reporter who attended featured the party the next day in the *New York Times.*

There are many times when business entertaining is better geared to this personel level. A small gathering may be the best way to welcome and please out-of-town clients or to woo important new contacts. A large affair may be overwhelming and not allow for easy conversation. And treating guests to a small party can be far more gracious than taking them out to dinner in a restaurant.

● **WHEN TO GO BIG.** When are a blockbuster party and a giant budget called for? An important new product launch might qualify. Parties at major industry trade shows or conventions are often worth extra effort, since companies usually compete for the same guests at these shows. And in some industries where extravagant parties are considered vital sales incentive or recruiting tools, entertaining is essential to remain competitive.

The *Wall Street Journal* reported recently on California's Silicon Valley, where companies competing for brain power do so in part by vying to stage the most exciting Christmas party. Apple Computer

has held a Dickens Christmas in a re-created English village, followed by a sumptuous dinner and a Chuck Berry concert. The same year, Computerland brought in the Fifth Dimension and, as they sang, launched thousands of balloons through a retractable roof over the ballroom. BR Communications, a telecommunications manufacturer, staged a carnival featuring dancers from Rio de Janeiro in silver beads and ostrich plumes, street performers, and trained parrots.

Extravagant? These companies insist there is a practical reason for the big-budget galas. In an industry where talent raids are frequent, new people are lured (and old employees retained) with salaries, stock options—and the promise of an exciting blowout at Christmas. It's hard to put a price tag on brain power.

Renting a private home can provide a unique setting for smaller gatherings without straining budgetary limits.

Officials at the Minolta Corporation were also firm in declaring that incentive rewards to top dealers, such as the elaborate Universal Studio party on page 68, pay for themselves many times over in generating extra sales efforts by the dealers.

TARGETING THE GUEST LIST

ONCE YOU HAVE ESTABLISHED THE purpose of your party and who you want to reach, everything else begins to fall into place—not only the size of your guest list, but who should be on it. Be sure that every appropriate department head is consulted about invitation lists. You may also want to contact salespeople for important contacts in their regions.

If your final list is very large or includes disparate groups of people, it may require more than one event to attain all your goals. A good example of multitargeting is the series of parties Barbara Boggs of Washington, Inc., planned for

Lufthansa when they wanted to announce a new direct flight from Washington to Frankfurt. The company's primary goal, to attract citywide publicity, was accomplished by arranging to have Lufthansa donate an antique plane to the Smithsonian Air and Space Museum. A big reception was held at the museum, with national and local travel and aviation press invited along with all the movers and shakers in Washington. The coverage was extensive.

But Lufthansa needed to reach specialized markets as well. A more selective guest list was compiled for a formal dinner set in the elegant quarters of the Smithsonian's National Portrait Gallery. Members of Congress and the Administration, heads of corporations and important law firms were invited, lured by the exclusivity of the occasion and the promise of a private performance by the Berlin Philharmonic.

Next, prominent Washington women were invited to lunch for a

Two-Way Benefit

When Crown Publishers joined forces with the Lighthouse Association for the Blind for the ball that launched Judith Krantz's best-seller Princess Daisy, both sponsors benefited. Few publishers could afford to hold a dinner dance for several hundred guests. Nor could a charity expect extensive media coverage for a typical benefit. Yet by working cooperatively to reproduce a ball from the pages of the book, both organizations accomplished their aims. The Lighthouse gained glamour, advance publicity, and many extra acceptances for their event. Free copies of the book contributed by the publisher were popular favors that also helped generate additional word-of-mouth publicity. And the media coverage was all either organization could have desired.

Lighthouse Benefit Ball Is One for the Book

Judith Krantz and David Mahoney, dancing; Marian Feldman, left, and Dolly Raisler in daisy-strewn ruffled Balmain dress.

showing of avant-garde German fashions. The intellectual community, including visitors such as exchange and graduate students, was invited to a debate between Henry Kissinger and the mayor of Berlin.

Each party was intended to showcase a specific aspect of German culture and to attract a carefully selected group of potential airline customers. Each group received a powerful personal reminder that Germany is a vital country—and that Lufthansa, the national airline, has convenient service direct from Washington.

Many companies would do well to follow the same entertaining strategy on a smaller scale, segmenting their events to appeal to specific groups. A magazine, for example, might invite young ad agency media buyers to a hot new dance club, but choose a more sedate setting for entertaining agency presidents.

WORKING WITH A LIMITED BUDGET

WHEN LARGE-SCALE ENTERTAINING seems called for but the budget is slim, imagination and creativity can still take you far. In a publishing company that puts out two or three hundred books each year, nonblockbuster books are often allocated very modest budgets. I've had to find ways to stretch them.

Sometimes this can be done most effectively through charity tie-ins (see box on facing page). I've also been able to cut costs by finding new restaurants or clubs that will give us a break on price or even donate their space in exchange for the publicity value of a high-profile event. Sometimes unexpected spaces can be obtained in return for publicity for the participants. Pub-

Stretching a Party Budget

- *Use a new restaurant or club that may donate space in exchange for publicity.*
- *Check out new office buildings or other large spaces such as showrooms that might be willing to lend their lobby in return for publicity.*
- *Serve hors d'oeuvres or a dinner or luncheon buffet-style to save on serving staff.*
- *Look for a charity tie-in that builds community good-will as well as provides a tax deduction.*
- *Think of using a private home, perhaps one belonging to a company executive.*
- *Offer wine or punch instead of having an open bar.*
- *Choose simple floral displays that emphasize drama rather than a profusion of flowers.*
- *Opt for an inexpensive entree such as chicken or paella rather than veal or beef.*
- *Remember that little things add up. Example: be sure the invitation does not require extra postage. Also consider using an arresting postcard as an invitation.*
- *Hire a disc jockey instead of a band.*

Time for Tea

The English have known it for a long time. In America, we are just learning to appreciate the graciousness of afternoon tea. At a time when many people are cutting back on alcohol, tea is a welcome break, a more intimate setting than a "power breakfast" or a luncheon, an opportunity for relaxed, quiet conversation.

Teas also are a savvy way to entertain stylishly on a limited budget. It is relatively inexpensive to set a generous tea table, adorned with handsome silver teapots and lush floral bouquets. The tea menu may be dainty or hearty. It might include sandwiches and a selection of desserts, traditional scones with heavy cream and jam, or tasty home-made muffins.

Whatever you serve, trays should be heaped high to give a feeling of plenty. A selection of teas allows guests to sample new blends. Soft music— a piano, a violin, or perhaps a harp—adds a civilized and restful note.

A generous display of teacakes, beautiful flowers, *opposite,* and an elegant tea service complete with samovar, *left,* looks opulent yet falls within a reasonable budget. Offer several different types of tea, including at least one herbal variety.

Striking gladiolus are a good choice for centerpieces when cost is a factor. The luminous bases are actually made of glass blocks, which were illuminated with tiny flashlights. The effect is atmospheric and arresting —all on a shoe-string.

licist Donna Gould of Workman Publishers held a very successful party for Rosemary Kent's *Texas Handbook* in a Ford showroom, offering Tex-Mex food, music, and rides in pickup trucks. The coverage was tremendous and the space, food, and rides were gratis, donated by a Ford dealer in return for the media exposure.

An innovative party planner can also help in cutting costs creatively. Caterer Gene Singletary helped the Miami Film Festival give a smashing fund-raiser on a tight budget. The festival's organizers wanted an "arty" party atmosphere. To supply it at little cost, Gene raided local junkyards in search of discarded refrigerators, had his staff scrub them down, and persuaded local artists to do custom paint jobs

ways to entertain, such as a wonderful breakfast, an afternoon tea, or a black-tie dessert and champagne party—all less expensive than the standard lunch or dinner and often a welcome change that attracts extra attention—and more acceptances.

ACCURATE BUDGET ESTIMATES

GET COMPLETE BUDGET ESTIMATES ON every aspect of the party before you make final decisions on your location and menu. Inexperienced party-givers are sometimes dismayed to find that it is not the food or the space but seemingly small details that boost costs beyond what they expected. They may remember the expense of printing invitations, but forget about the cost of addressing and mailing them. Insurance, security, sales tax, service charges, and tips must also be figured into your budget; they add significantly to the total.

When you check on insurance, it is wise to compare the caterers' cost with the rate the company can get on its own. Sometimes you come out better using your company's own insurance carrier.

Always leave yourself a contingency allowance for last-minute items you never expected, such as additional security personnel or sound equipment, or the possibility of extra guests. Such things frequently come up, even with the most careful planning.

When all the costs are in, consider carefully before you cut back on items such as invitations, flowers, or lighting. These are not just details, but important elements in the event's overall design. Better to serve more simply than risk spoiling the party's ambience.

on each one. Using dry ice as a refrigerant, he stocked the shelves with food so guests could help themselves. Each time a refrigerator door was opened, waves of white vapor filled the air, giving the party a funky sense of surprise.

There are also many practical ways to cut costs, such as serving buffet style to cut down on service staff or looking for innovative

A Happy Anniversary at Caramoor

THE 150TH ANNIVERSARY of this venerable New York law firm was an impressive milestone—one deserving of an extravagant, big-budget celebration. The sylvan setting and lush feeling of elegance were an eloquent way to express the firm's gratitude to longstanding clients. The party also served to solidify relationships with newer clients, and deepen the commitment of their partners.

WHO

KELLY, DRYE AND WARREN, ATTORNEYS AT LAW

WHAT

DINNER DANCE FOR 800

WHERE

THE CARAMOOR ESTATE, KATONAH, NEW YORK

WHY

150TH ANNIVERSARY CELEBRATION

The location was Caramoor, an exceptional estate about one hour from New York City. Caramoor's canopied Venetian theater, adorned with Greek and Roman marble columns that once graced a fifteenth-century Italian garden, is the site of a noted summer music festival. To add to its beauty, the theater is set amid one hundred acres of woodland, lawns, and gardens.

The idea of using the theater as a party setting came from one of the firm's partners, who serves on the board of directors and knew that a limited number of private events are allowed there. Abigail Kirsch Culinary Productions was chosen for the event because her firm has served the Music Festival's annual benefit gala as well as events for other corporate clients on the premises, so the staff was also familiar with transforming the theater from concert arena to party

French service adds a touch of sophistication to any catered affair, *above*. The Mediterranean architecture of the main house added interest and elegance to the setting, *opposite*. *Overleaf:* With the right lighting, an ordinary tent can take on a magical glow. Here, strings of tiny white lights nestle in greenery.

space, no small undertaking.

The black-tie occasion called for an elegant menu. From the caterer's point of view, it also dictated food that would require a minimum of refrigeration during the afternoon and would be appealing served at room temperature. The client received three sample menus. Their final menu culled selections from all three. On the evening of the party they were ready with 790 veal dinners—plus 9 kosher meals and one Pritikin diet.

Since the dinner location was some distance from New York, the law firm appreciated the functions of a full-service caterer who helped plan every aspect of a party, including suggesting the right florist and

Holding an important dinner out-doors, *top*, means keeping guests comfortable regardless of weather. Covered walkways, *above*, were constructed between the cocktail and dinner areas so no one need get wet in case of showers. Having a separate tent for cocktails, *opposite*, allowed the waiters to set up for dinner without inter-rupting conversations.

A superb outdoor setting extends party space and creates spaces such as this garden, *above,* for special quiet moments. Music, candles, and sparkling columns, *opposite,* created a magical atmosphere for a post-dinner concert.

band for the occasion. The caterer even furnished scale drawings of table placement to allow the firm to make seating assignments without extra trips to the site.

After dinner, a short, warm speech from one of the partners told of the firm's long history and ended with a toast and thanks to all. As a fitting Caramoor musical finale, there was a twenty-minute concert by the Orchestra of St. Luke's, followed by dancing.

Caramoor Menu

BY ABIGAIL KIRSCH
CULINARY
PRODUCTIONS

*Passed Hot and Cold
Hors d'Oeuvres*

*Gulf Shrimp and Sea Scallops in a
Citrus Vinaigrette*

*Roast Loin of Veal with Apricot
Currant Chutney*

*Wild Rice with Finely Diced Red
and Yellow Bell Pepper*

Medley of Summer Vegetables

*Vacherin Filled with Strawberries,
Raspberries, and Blueberries
Served with Chantilly Cream*

*French Roast, Decaffeinated Coffee,
and Tea*

Choosing a Theme

WITH PURPOSE and budget determined, the next step in planning a party is setting a theme, a central idea to give creative focus to menus, music, decor, and entertainment. Parties lacking a unifying theme are seldom memorable events. And though many people think a theme party means props or gimmicks, a backdrop is only one aspect of creating a successful theme—and sometimes scenery is not needed at all.

Chapter

3

A creative theme has more to do with mood than with props. It is an overall vision of what you want guests to feel when they arrive, a springboard for developing the special touches and ambience that will set your party apart.

The theme can be as simple as the summer freshness of the Chicago outdoor party on page 108, or as funky as the DecaDance theme on page 190, which created atmosphere entirely through color scheme, table decor, and menu. Whatever the spirit of the occasion, establishing a distinctive mood takes a party out of the ordinary.

WHERE TO GET IDEAS

IDEAS FOR THEMES CAN COME FROM many sources. Sometimes an unusual menu can be the inspiration for decor that brings alive the flavor of another country. Lansdowne Catering staged a gilded Taj Majal buffet for three hundred in the garden of the Textile Museum in Washington with a menu of Indian foods that was far more original

and enjoyable than the standard no-theme cocktail buffet. Lobbyist Nancy Reynolds, a great party-giver, came up with a Basque Barbecue, a fund-raiser for Senator Paul Laxalt, whose origins are Basque. She had lamb flown in from the Basque country to be cooked on the spit, creating a menu and ambience that was different and welcome.

One of the more original foreign themes was set at a *Dr. Zhivago* party that was held in an unexpected and inspired location, an old church. A menu of Russian delicacies was combined with falling snow, costumed dancers, Russian music, and giant sunflowers everywhere to provide a contagious festivity that was irresistible.

Often your company's products will suggest the party's theme. That is often the case for me with books, and it was the elegant image of the product that called for the setting and decor of the Givenchy party shown on page 180.

Sometimes the season or the calendar suggests a theme. It might be a fanciful occasion like Ground Hog Day or Flag Day, or you may be able to add a fresh look to a familiar idea like a July Fourth celebration or a romantic Valentine's Day ball.

● **LOOK FOR A NEW TWIST.** Often one unexpected touch is all it takes to give new life to an old idea. Robert

A Night in the Jungles of Boston

Pith helmets for each guest and hosts dressed in jungle togs, *above and right,* made party-goers feel they were on safari. Steamy dry ice, *below,* camouflaged unsightly hotel drapes and added atmosphere as did huge wild animal cutouts, *opposite.*

Even landmarks have to face up to changing times. Boston is filled with new hotels and interesting historic party spaces. When the tradition-rich Palmer House Hotel wanted to let their patrons know that they could still compete, they did it with a high-spirited theme party that transformed the stately grand ballroom into a jungle.

"Five years ago we would have entertained this group with an elegant cocktail party and maybe a little dancing," says Lee Ferris, field director of marketing. "But today that is no longer enough. People are looking for something extra at a party. We have to show them we can deliver it, even in a hotel ballroom."

Here's what it took a party designer to transform a ballroom into a jungle:

- life-size wooden cutouts of giraffe, elephant, lion, zebra, and tiger
- 100 yards of rope
- 100 bamboo poles
- 12 sections of palm thatching
- 8-foot tiki pole
- 2 stuffed parrots
- 1 stuffed jaguar
- imported alligator parts
- 3 live birds
- live tropical fish
- artificial grass
- rubber snakes, tarantulas, spiders
- inflatable alligators, zebras, giraffes, spiders
- large roll of brown paper
- rubber cobwebs
- skeleton
- 5-foot swimming pool
- environmental sound tapes
- fish line, wire, masking tape
- Florals: 75 stems of halaconia, 30 large allium, 200 anthurium, 144 birds of paradise, 60 monkshood, 40 ginger flowers, 12 protea, 50 waleback foliage, 75 monstera, 500 stems varied large tropical foliage.
- Plants: 12 14-foot ficus trees, 6 bamboo palms, 6 kentia palms, 25 schefflera, 20 yucca, 15 peace lilies, 10 large corn plants, 6 Dracaena marginata; 15 arbacola, 6 China Doll; 12 8-inch hibiscus, 20 assorted tropical plants.

Period fixtures, jars of doughnut holes, and photographs of Churchill all contributed to the feeling of a 1940s British diner at Crown's party for Judith Krantz.

Marston, Inc., a New York public relations firm, makes an annual Saint Patrick's Day party for the business press stand out by hiring bagpipers to parade through the room after the event gets underway. For newcomers, the parade is a surprise that always brings laughs and cheers; for old-timers at the party, it is eagerly anticipated year after year. It leaves people smiling and sets the tone for a happy event.

People vie for invitations to the Mardi Gras event held annually by Louisiana's senators and congress-men at a Washington hotel. The special lure? The best chefs from New Orleans and Shreveport, flown up to supply fabulous food for the occasion in person.

The big daddy of all Mardi Gras celebrations may well be the one Mary Micucci of Along Came Mary staged for the World Film Market in Hollywood. Mary virtually re-created the city of New Orleans on a 30,000-foot sound stage. Seafood was served against a setting of wharves, pilings, and fishermen's shacks, while Cajun

Merry Holiday Parties

One type of theme party that almost every company has to give is the annual Christmas/Holiday Party. It can be (and most often is) a big bore. What can be done to make it fun? How can you stay within a reasonable budget, make employees feel valued, create an atmosphere of fun, and get people within the company mixing with each other? Here are some suggestions:

• Discuss your company's personality with the caterer or party planner. Is your image conservative or funky? Do your employees like to dance, or would chamber music be more appropriate? Is sushi too adventurous, or would roast beef and turkey be more fitting?

• Vary the location, music, and menu from year to year. People like to be surprised.

• Have as many people as possible checking coats since most guests will arrive at the same time. Consider positioning carolers, classical music, or mimes in the check area to distract people and set the tone for the rest of the event.

• Food stations encourage good traffic flow and create a fun atmosphere. People are forced to bump into each other and mingle with coworkers from different departments.

• Still or video photography of the party in progress is fun and can be used in years to come for a nostalgic look at the company's past.

• Decide in advance which executives will make speeches, when, and how long they will be, and whether or not they require a hand microphone and/or a podium. Coordinate with the entertainment people so they get the guests to quiet down and listen.

• Don't skimp on entertainment. It can make or break the party. In my opinion, it's more important than the food or the drinks. Spend time in advance watching a video of the group or seeing them live. If you can't do either of these, check out references carefully.

• I prefer scheduling lunches that go into late afternoon the week before Christmas. Some companies prefer evening parties but usually employees feel so frantic that an evening becomes another burden. Avoid weekends totally unless an executive is hosting an intimate small-scale party in his or her home.

• I think an open bar is the best way to go. There are so many tastes within one company it is difficult to narrow the choices down. But if you have to cut in budget, this is where I'd look to reduce expenses.

---

specialties, hush puppies, jambalaya, and po' boy sandwiches were found along facades of Bourbon Street, accurate right down to the neon signs. This was an elaborate party, but it wasn't just expensive stage dressing that made it work. It was the authenticity of every detail that delighted guests and helped make them feel they had been magically transported to New Orleans for the night. (Mary actually traveled to New Orleans to be sure her backdrops, recipes, and music, even the *beignets* and French coffee, would be absolutely right.)

• **PICKING UP FROM THE PROS.** Your clipping file containing write-ups of wonderful big parties like these can be an invaluable resource, since their various elements can often be emulated on a smaller scale.

Parties Plus in Los Angeles won an award from *Special Events* magazine for the gigantic opening they staged for the Westside Pavilion, a party that covered three floors of the three-block shopping complex and took guests on a mini–world tour. The first floor featured foods from Europe, the second floor offered a taste of the Orient. But it was the top floor that guests enjoyed most. Here they "traveled"

A personalized SAG card followed by a Hollywood screen test drew guests into the excitement of a movie back lot at the Minolta party. A Ronald Reagan look-alike posed with guests for photos.

across America for regional desserts —blackberry-apple pie, strawberry shortcake, and the favorite surprise of all: eight grandmothers serving chocolate cake, cookies, and cold milk from a vintage 1940s Midwestern kitchen.

Many ideas might be borrowed from the "Jingle Bells and Coconuts" Christmas party staged by Gene Singletary for Burger King in a downtown plaza in Miami. The evening began with champagne served aboard Miami's new overhead Metro system. It was a short stroll from the Metro stop to the new Art Plaza, where a whimsical mix of tropical and polar decor awaited—palm trees with Christmas lights, six-foot flamingos with Santa Claus beards and hats. Machete-wielding waiters chopped coconuts, laced the milk with rum, and served them up with straws. Singletary and his staff, six-foot spatulas in hand, cooked paella in a giant nine-foot-round paella pan. Alternating bands offered continuous music from rock to '50s to

blues; a host of street performers, circus acts, and actors wearing giant heads of movie stars and characters from "Miami Vice" kept everyone laughing. Something was happening everywhere guests looked, and they were invited to get into the fun—to dance, to sample the unusual fare, to clown with the clowns.

INVOLVE THE GUESTS

A SURE WAY TO GET GUESTS INTO THE spirit of your theme is to make them active participants. The highlight of an American convention held in Melbourne, Australia, was a party modeled after that city's big annual event, the Melbourne Cup horse race. The feel of the racetrack was re-created in a Hyatt Hotel ballroom with hedges, outdoor tables and chairs, bright umbrellas, and waiters dressed in brightly striped jockey silks. The big surprise was tote boards at the end of the room displaying race odds— and numbers takers standing by ready to take bets.

Each guest found $300 in play money at his or her place and a witty racing card with entrants whose names represented members of the group. Between each course at dinner, actual footage from past competitions was shown on a big screen. There was much cheering from the winners, gnashing of teeth by the losers, lots of mixing and mingling—and everyone had a wonderful time.

WHEN TO BRING IN THE EXPERTS

THERE ARE SOME BIG-BUDGET THEME parties that succeed in creating a mood by their opulence and beauty. Big benefits in particular often stage elaborate scenes such as

a winter wonderland, an indoor garden, a circus, or a page out of the Arabian Nights. In New York, parties like this can run anywhere from $25,000 to $200,000. I would never undertake such an event unless I could afford to hire someone who knows how to create not just scenery but extraordinary ambience, a top party designer whose business is special effects. You can see the work of one of them at the *Vanity Fair* party on page 44. The best way to find such a talented designer is to check in big-city newspaper style pages and in publications such as *Women's Wear*

Daily, Town & Country, or city magazines. *Special Events* magazine, a trade publication in Los Angeles, is another source of stories about exceptional events. The best designers are written up frequently. Watch these publications and clip articles for your party file so you'll know the right party geniuses to call on when you need them.

Once you have found your wizards, allow them to *use* their originality. The best parties often are those where the host has been willing to take risks, to give a party designer freedom to create something wonderfully original.

Costumed spacemen serving dessert from smoking trays added an element of science fiction to the Minolta party.

A Trip to the Thirties with Vanity Fair

THE PARTY OF THE YEAR. *Vanity Fair* magazine wanted no less for their fifth-anniversary gala, a party that would herald the success of the famous Thirties magazine's stylish revival in the manner of that period. To bring it off with a flourish, they counted on the wizardry of a top party designer, Robert Isabell—and he did not let them down. The evening had all the glitter and energy of a prohibition-era speakeasy.

Isabell brought back to life the Diamond Horseshoe, a nightclub that was the toast of New York in the 1930s, when the original *Vanity Fair* was in its heyday. Five hundred guests, including a who's who of Hollywood headliners and New York's beautiful people,

WHO

VANITY FAIR MAGAZINE

WHAT

BLACK-TIE BUFFET DINNER-DANCE

WHERE

CENTURY PARAMOUNT HOTEL, NEW YORK CITY

WHY

FIFTH-ANNIVERSARY CELEBRATION

danced on until the wee hours in a space made spectacular by Isabell's transformation.

Once a Thirties motif was decided on, finding a large space other than a standard hotel ballroom was the first challenge. The deserted basement area that was once a nightclub hadn't been used for years and was in "dastardly shape," according to Jean Karlson, *Vanity Fair*'s promotion director.

But Isabell knew exactly what was needed to do the job. He made good use of the glamorous elements that remained from the past, bringing out the curving staircase, chandeliers, and fluted columns with paint and lighting. Rich fabrics added elegance. Photographs from issues of the vintage *Vanity Fair* lined the stairway walls. The room was filled with real palm trees, rigged to the ceiling to look as though they were rooted in their own grove.

As guests arrived, dancers in Carmen Miranda feathers and conga ruffles stood along the stairway, shimmying to Afro-Latin rhythms that set the stage for danc-

Gold spraypaint and dramatic lighting transformed a dreary deserted room, *above,* into a glittering nightclub, *opposite.* This kind of transformation requires imagination, creativity, and technical know-how. Check before-and-after photographs of party designers' work before choosing with whom you will work.

Right and below:
Celebrities draw publicity and glamour to a party, but be careful to limit and control photographers and/or television crew; celebrity guests like the limelight, but they also value their privacy on social occasions.

Vanity Fair **editor Tina Brown,** *opposite***, gave her personal thanks to magazine supporters against a backdrop of some of her most memorable issues. Prior to the party she had a dry run of her speech to be assured the acoustics were correct.**

ing from the first moment.

While Isabell handled the design of the room, party planner Karin Bacon scouted appropriate entertainment. She came up with a winner in Kit McClure's all-girl band, done up in marcelled wigs and Kewpie-doll lips. Their music ran the gamut from jitterbug to rock-and-roll, keeping the crowd on its feet well into the night.

Every carefully orchestrated detail of this party contributed to an overall mood the *Hollywood Reporter* called "a Byzantine palm court of gilded glitz . . . thundering with East Coast energy"—in other words, just what the hosts had ordered: the party of the year.

Vanity Fair Dinner Menu

BY GLORIOUS FOOD

HORS D'OEUVRES

Smoked Salmon on Black Bread
with Dill

Cheese Straws

Toasted Almonds

BUFFET

Roasted Legs of Veal with
Basil Sauce

Vol-au-Vents of Tortellini in Black
Truffle Cream Sauce

Marinated Baby Vegetables

Shrimp, Tomato, Fennel, and
Arugula Salad

Assorted Cheeses and
Country Breads

DESSERT

Fifth-Anniversary Petit Fours

Glorious Brownies and
Pecan Squares

Glorious Cookies

Baskets of Long-Stemmed
Strawberries

Coffee

A bevy of blond musicians, *above,* added off-beat humor and delight to an evening full of surprises. When Latin rhythms rang out at midnight, vividly costumed dancers led everyone in a joyous Conga line, *opposite.*

Selecting a Caterer and Party Planner

CHOOSING the professionals who will help you bring your event to life may be the most important party decision you will make. Even if you have a location in mind, it can prove helpful to interview the professionals first; they may change your mind by suggesting original spaces that aren't widely known. A creative planner can also help you clarify and improve on a party theme and hire the appropriate professionals.

Chapter 4

An important consideration is how much help you need. If you want a central location and are thinking of doing most of the planning yourself, you may be happy working with the staff of a convenient hotel. If you want to consider a more unusual space, you will require a caterer. In either case you will have to establish whether the hotel or caterer can be relied on to take care of finding other suppliers such as florists, lighting experts, and musicians—or whether you should use the services of a professional planner or party designer whose business it is to take care of these details.

Your budget, your experience at party giving, and your familiarity with the city in which you are working will also help determine the right choices.

Begin by interviewing both hotel banquet managers and independent caterers and take a look at the spaces they recommend. Each has pros and cons; you will be deciding which is better suited to your needs (see box, following page).

THE ROLE OF THE PARTY PLANNER

WHEN YOU ARE GIVING AN IMPORTANT party and need a fresh and unusual touch, you may also want to interview a relatively new kind of professional, the party planner.

A party planner functions as a time-saving organizer who will scout locations, come up with theme or decor ideas, and then hire the best people to take care of all the elements—food, flowers, decoration, lighting, and music—necessary to realize it. A planner can take a lot of decisions and worry off your shoulders.

Some caterers who call themselves full-service caterers also function as party planners. Some contract with outside suppliers, others are large operations with their own in-house staffs for lighting and decor as well as food. In many cities, full-service caterers are some of the top planners, so don't overlook them when conducting your first round of interviews. Whether to select a full-service caterer or a party planner depends

Hotel Banquet Facilities versus Independent Caterers

HOTEL PROS

- *Convenient locations, especially important during conventions.*
- *Personnel experienced at handling large groups.*
- *Facilities for cabs or parking, coat check, rest rooms, etc.*
- *Rooms of varying sizes to fit most groups.*
- *Safe choice—you know what you are getting.*

HOTEL CONS

- *Limited menus—most hotels require that you use their in-house catering service, which may not be as creative as an outside caterer.*
- *Drink packages—hotels rarely permit clients to bring in their own liquor, which can help keep the bill under control.*
- *Institutional or unimaginative spaces that may require additional decoration expense.*

CATERER PROS

- *You get more for less money.*
- *Much greater flexibility in locations.*
- *Menus are often more creative.*
- *Lighting and decor are more imaginative.*
- *Clients usually can supply their own alcohol, at retail for substantial savings.*

CATERER CONS

- *Interviewing several different candidates is time consuming.*
- *Logistics are more complicated.*
- *Greater risk is involved.*
- *Transportation arrangements may be difficult.*
- *Unexpected last-minute expenses may arise.*

on your specific needs. Advantages of full-service caterers are:
- you deal with just one person
- you can see examples of the full range of services you will be contracting for.

Advantages of independent party planners:
- when an unusual menu is called for, a party planner's knowledge of a wide number of caterers enables him or her to find someone right for your needs, from sushi to sirloin
- when a hotel is the most convenient location for your event, a planner may be able to come up with innovative decorating ideas that will make your party stand out even in a standard setting. He or she may also be able to negotiate with the hotel for a better

price or more interesting menu and can oversee the service personnel for you.

Whichever you choose, your party professional should have inside knowledge of the particular city and the connections to get you into interesting spaces you wouldn't ordinarily have access to. Knowledgeable planners make it their business to know all the city's resources, from where to find the hottest jazz band to which florist rents the biggest palm trees. As frequent customers, they can often get better prices than you could on your own. More important, they can buy you peace of mind, a priceless commodity when you're working in a strange city.

Planners charge in different ways for their services. Some have a flat

Ringing the Bell for Weddings

Martha Stewart was already a culinary superstar when we launched her book Weddings *at the American Booksellers Association convention in New Orleans. But we wanted to make it clear that this was going to be the biggest of all her best-sellers—and party planner Robert O'Brien of Capricho was instrumental in creating a party to get that message across.*

First, he changed my mind about location, convincing me that the old U.S. Mint building was better than the Southern plantation I had in mind. While it also had old New Orleans ambience, the building was more centrally located and had many levels and a courtyard offering opportunities for the diversity of moods we wanted to achieve.

Then he came up with magical touches far beyond my expectations—wrapping the building like a wedding gift, posting gospel singers outside to greet guests as they arrived, using music from string quartet to blues to dance band to draw the crowd from one area to another. Other treats for guests

were models wearing fabulous Pat Carr bridal gowns and a display of stunning wedding cakes, including one Martha had made herself.

Refreshments were champagne and dessert only—but what desserts! Robert and Martha had persuaded the city's top chefs to participate. Each participating restaurant had a table, and many of the celebrity chefs were there in person.

These innovative features brought extensive media coverage, including TV crews from "Entertainment Tonight" and "Good Morning, America" and articles in the New York Times, *the* Washington Post, *and* Vanity Fair.

No one left the party unaware that a special book was on the way. Early orders were so heavy that this $50 book was in a third printing and on the best-seller list even before the official publication date. I know no better example of the marketing power of creative entertaining—or the contribution that a talented party planner can make when you give him some freedom.

Perfect Surroundings' preliminary sketch for the Parker House Safari Party helped both client and planner visualize what the end result would be, always a good idea when an elaborate effect is being planned.

fee while others charge a percentage of the total cost for their time and expertise. Full-service planner-caterers who employ their own cooking and decorating staffs usually just factor their planning services into the total cost.

The method of billing does not really matter, as long as you are clear from the start what the total cost will be. When I am working outside of my own city, I have found the services of a party planner well worth the extra fees. These professionals absorb a lot of the anxiety of orchestrating a party long distance.

If you come to a planner with a theme in mind, he or she may be able to bring it to life in wonderfully original ways. Creative planners can help produce events

beyond anything you might have conceived on your own. If you have not been able to come up with a theme, a planner can suggest one; just be sure it is in keeping with your company's image and goals, not just for the sake of novelty.

It is even more crucial to have good references for a planner than for a caterer, since the usefulness of a planner is often a matter of contacts, taste, and creativity, which can be less tangible than the ability to prepare good food.

● **THE PARTY DESIGNER.** One other type of professional to consider for really major events is the party designer. Designers specialize in creating special effects with the right lighting, props, flowers, and decor. When the budget permits, a talented designer can create party

magic, completely transforming any space, including a staid hotel ballroom. Party designers usually contract only for the decor and atmosphere of a party; they do not get involved in hiring caterers or musicians as a party planner would.

MAKING A CHOICE

WHATEVER TYPE OF PROFESSIONAL you choose, the big challenge facing a novice is finding a talented and reliable person to work with. Before making any final decisions, you should compare and consider several candidates. Again, one thing I strongly recommend is keeping a clipping file on outstanding parties that you read about and a file of names of people whose creative work you have seen, as discussed on page 7. See the box on page 59 for other ways to find competent party professionals.

Almost always, a few names will come up over and over again in your research, and the selection process should begin with phone calls to these people. If you are inexperienced at giving parties, say so. A real professional is accustomed to guiding novices and will know the right questions to ask *you.* You will be ahead of the game if you are prepared with the simple basic information professionals need—the same basic information you will already have determined within your company:

• the purpose of your party.
• the type and number of guests to be invited.
• your budget.

Caterers tell me that some clients almost deliberately resist revealing their budgets. They do this in hopes that the caterer will come up with a figure lower than what they can actually afford. This can be a mistake, since every caterer has a range of menus from modest to lavish, with prices to match. You

A full-service caterer is well-equipped to handle the logistical problems that can arise outside of a controlled setting.

How to Find Party Professionals

- *Ask friends or business associates for names of people they have used and would recommend.*
- *Call the food or life-style editors of the local newspaper for recommendations.*
- *In an unfamiliar city, check back issues of the city magazine for articles on local catering and parties. The people featured are usually well regarded in the city.*
- *Solicit the top florists in town for suggestions.*
- *Contact public relations firms that give a lot of parties for recommendations.*
- *Approach the local convention bureau for suggestions.*
- *If you have already selected a location, ask the manager for names of caterers who have worked there before.*

may simply be getting a quote for the firm's low-budget menu. If you aren't sure of your budget, it is better to say so and ask for a range of prices and a sample menu for each. When comparing bids, don't ever assume that menus will be similar until you see them spelled out in detail—in writing.

Another thing the professionals need to know is the desired mood of the party: formal or informal, traditional or offbeat. Bill Hansen, a Miami party planner, says he finds it helpful to ask inexperienced clients, "What are you imagining?"

● **THE RIGHT QUESTIONS.** On the phone, you will also want to ask some questions of your own, questions that will immediately give you a preliminary sense of the candidate's suitability for your needs. Remember that your needs may vary depending on whether you are most concerned with the quality of the food at a sit-down dinner or the originality of the decor for a theme party. The same person may not be the best candidate for both categories. I generally ask potential

Clear advance instructions are an important ingredient in a smoothly run event. Good planners make sure every staff member understands his role with a preparty briefing, *opposite.*

caterers the following questions:

- how many years have you been in business?
- who are some of your regular clients and what types of parties have you done for them?
- how varied are your menus? Can I see or sample the food?
- are you licensed to serve liquor?
- what are your special strengths?
- do you have your own staff or do you use outside people for flowers, lighting, and decor? If you use outsiders, who are they?
- what are your rates? Is there a minimum? Are service and gratuities included?

The same questions apply to party planners, except that I ask about the caterers they use most often rather than about their menus.

If the answers to my questions sound promising, I ask for an information kit, some sample menus from caterers, and some references. I *always* call the references. Then I set up interviews, asking to be shown potential party spaces as well as menus.

If I am scouting a new city, I plan a minimum of two days, allowing half a day for each interview and trying to see at least three people as well as a couple of hotels. It takes at least half a day to look at spaces and get a feel for whether you can work with someone, at least an hour in a hotel. Meeting three caterers and/or planners is usually sufficient to enable me to make comparisons without wearing myself out, but I'll add extra time if there is someone who sounds too good to pass up.

In personal interviews, I ask to see slides or photographs of parties the firm has done in the past. Many

When construction on Houston's Heritage Plaza fell behind schedule, Sharon Graham's staff found themselves preparing dinner for 300 under the most primitive conditions.

Creating a Kitchen

Using an unconventional or an outdoor space means serving large numbers of people from a makeshift kitchen—sometimes from a cook tent, sometimes from an empty room. Caterers have to bring every kind of equipment needed to cook and store food—and often their own power and water supplies as well.

If you do have your heart set on a space without a proper kitchen, Abigail Kirsch offers these tips for selecting and working with your caterer:

• *Hire the most experienced caterer you can find (and afford); he will be better prepared to deal with any emergency that comes up.*

• *Keep the menu light and simple. If possible, choose room temperature dishes that can be prepared in advance, and don't expect your caterer to serve elaborate dishes with fragile sauces. Also avoid perishables like mayonnaise and ice creams or sorbets, which must be refrigerated until the last second.*

• *If your party is held in the spring or summer, an excellent menu option is chicken, fish, or vegetables cooked on a grill or hibachi. They can be set up in a tent, visible to the guests, or behind the scenes. Just check to be sure the smoke will not intrude on the event.*

• *Double-check that the caterer has assessed his electrical requirements for heating units, lights, fans, and refrigeration well in advance of the event.*

• *Make sure the space has a water source and an area of level ground for the work areas.*

Party Planners West spent a day and a half wiring and lighting an airport hangar for Crown's Judith Krantz party, *above,* bringing lighting into a space that literally had none. A well-connected party planner can introduce you to private spaces you could never have access to on your own, such as the mansion, *right,* that Washington, Inc., secured for a convention dinner.

firms also have videos of their parties. When assessing a hotel, photographs can give you a sense of their talent for presentation and whether they have been able to do something out of the ordinary within the confines of a standard banquet room.

● **TASTE, IMAGINATION, CONNECTIONS.**
When I interview professionals, I am looking for three things: taste, imagination, and connections. One of the reasons we like working with Washington, Inc., in Washington, D.C., for example, is that its staff members are so well connected in this very political city. They can get us entree into private clubs and homes that aren't available to the average person or even to most caterers. That makes our parties more desirable.

Another way to judge a professional is by how well he or she can help you to visualize the party concretely. I like someone who can walk me through a space, showing me where the bar will go, where music will be, and how the party traffic will flow. In public places like hotels or museums, disposing of coats is not usually a problem, but an experienced planner knows that in a private home or club

placement matters. Putting the coat check too near the door can clog the entrance, while putting it too far away may leave people wandering, unsure of where to go. I feel reassured when I hear someone tell me exactly what they have in mind for this kind of detail, and even what extra provisions they have made for emergencies—such as having a place to store umbrellas in case of rain. It shows me they are aware of the important logistics of a party and can anticipate possible problems before they occur.

Larger firms with extensive cooking staffs routinely book several parties for busy dates, so the

head man or woman may only appear briefly to scan the preparations at each party. This need not be a matter of concern, so long as you meet the chef and party manager for your event in advance. With smaller firms, I generally like to ask how many other events the caterer has scheduled for my date, to be sure he or she isn't taking on more than he or she can handle.

● **EXPERIENCE COUNTS.** If your party will be held in an unusual space, ask whether the caterer is experienced in setting up and serving from a portable kitchen. It is always reassuring to know that the person in charge of your party is

familiar with the space and its requirements. I would be nervous about working with any caterer who does not ask to see an unfamiliar space before planning a menu for you.

Make sure the catering firm you choose is large and experienced enough to handle all aspects of your party. Smaller mom-and-pop operations working out of their own homes may create wonderful food, but may not have necessary insurance or liquor licenses or be inspected by the health department. They may be suitable for at-home entertaining where you are in control of these things but all wrong

Transformation completed, the empty hangar boasted a collage of famous nightclubs like the Brown Derby, Trocadero, and Coconut Grove, testament to the party planner's skill and imagination.

for events held in a public space.

Be wary also of hiring a trendy restaurant chef to cater a party in another location. Off-premises catering is not at all the same as cooking in one's own well-equipped kitchen, and sometimes a star chef is a flop under less-controlled conditions.

In my own city, where I have a chance to sample a caterer's offerings firsthand, I'll often take a chance on new young caterers or planners who seem creative. I've gotten terrific results from some of these firms. Talented newcomers tend to have fresh ideas, and because they are eager to build their reputations, they often try harder —and may throw in extras for free to ensure a great party as well as repeat business.

Out of town, I have to depend more heavily on experience and references. And when I asked top

professionals their advice on choosing among several seemingly qualified candidates, experience was the single most important credential stressed. It even helps to know that the caterer's waiters have experience, that they have worked for the caterer before and worked together as a team.

Julie Loshin of Parties Plus in Los Angeles cautions, "What happens if there is a problem? Can the caterer or planner cope? Emergencies do happen. One night, the rental company forgot to deliver dinner plates with the client's order. We had a quick conference and decided to present the food nouvelle style on salad plates in three small servings instead of on one larger dinner plate. We washed dishes like crazy between courses, but the hostess never even knew anything was wrong. She loved the presentation. A less-experienced caterer might have panicked and the dinner would have been ruined."

● **OTHER CONSIDERATIONS.** If the food to be served is your top priority, you may want to sample the caterer's fare before making a final selection. Caterers have different ways of providing food tastings for prospective clients. Some stage sampling luncheons regularly, and some restaurateur-caterers invite potential clients to taste their fare in the restaurant. Others may offer to prepare an individual sample menu.

I prefer to attend an actual party done by the caterer whenever possible, since you can't always judge party presentation or large-scale service from a private lunch or tasting. In the long run, though, I still find references are the best reassurance if you can't attend a party.

There are many good party professionals in almost every city, and I often see more than one person who seems able to do a fine job for us. When the decision is tough, it boils down to my instinct and the rapport I feel with the person. I want someone I feel comfortable with and feel I can trust. And I always prefer to work with people who show energy, a sense of fun, and a passion for their work. You won't get a wonderful party from a boring person. It takes genuine enthusiasm and creativity to produce a lively party. Their spirit and the way they talk about their work are major factors in my final decision.

THE PROPOSAL/CONTRACT

AFTER YOU HAVE NARROWED DOWN your choices, ask for a detailed proposal on the party costs. Discuss the questions that follow with your caterer beforehand so the answers can be reflected in his proposal.

If you are working with a hotel, question whether a separate fee will be charged for use of the room in addition to the food. Sometimes this fee is negotiable.

If the menu is not clearly spelled out, here are examples of items you might want clarified:

- if shrimp is listed among the hors d'oeuvres, how many shrimps per person are allowed? And what size—small, medium, jumbo?
- how many canapés per person?
- what kind of salad ingredients will be used—tossed greens or more exotic fare?
- on a dessert buffet, exactly what will the choices be?
- at a sit-down dinner, will there be plate service, meaning a plate prepared in advance in the kitchen, or more formal and elegant French service, foods served onto your plate from a tray by the waiter?
- exactly what brand and quality of wine will be used?
- will wine be poured from bottles or carafes?
- will the caterer also supply non-alcoholic drinks?

Also ask for specific details about the rentals:

- will tablecloths be white or colored?
- will there be an undercloth too?
- what kind of chairs will be used?
- will the china be plain white, colored, or gold-rimmed?
- what type of glasses will be used?
- will serving trays be silver or glass?
- who absorbs the cost of broken dishes or burned linens?

Other things to be reflected in the proposal:

- exactly how many tables will be set up?

Careful attention to details is the hallmark of a topnotch planner or caterer.

• how many people will be seated at each table?
• how many waiters are allotted per table? How many busboys?
• will a floor plan of the tables be provided so that you can set up seating?

If you are having more than two hundred people, ask how many kitchens will be set up, how many buffets, and how many bars. It is important also to ask for a breakdown of the staff—how many there will be at the bar, how many serving, bussing, and cleaning up in the kitchen. You should make it clear if you want your party generously staffed—and be prepared to pay the difference.

If you are hiring a band, you will want to know how many instruments are in the band, exactly how many hours they will play, and how frequent and how long their breaks will be. Ask in advance whether the band will stay on if the party extends beyond the time limit and at what cost.

The questions don't end there. Here are a few other details you should know:
• what will the waiters wear?
• what kind of flowers will be used in the centerpieces?
• who will check coats and where?

• who will be responsible for providing valet parking service?
• how many hours will the caterer remain to take care of cleanup?
• when will rentals be picked up? Who will be responsible until then?
• what kind of insurance coverage does the caterer have? Do you need additional coverage?
• who will take care of security?
• is the contract sufficient for insurance and security or do you need a separate agreement?
• who will supply the liquor? The bartender? The setups?

Note that some bids come in for food only, without a bar estimate, making them seem lower than they actually are. Be sure you have a price for the bar. If you do purchase the liquor yourself, as is often the case, find out whether the caterer will provide mixers and setups. Factor in these additional costs when comparing bids. (See page 132 for guidelines on stocking a bar.)

All of these things affect the bottom-line price, and all should be clearly spelled out. Ask lots of questions—and get the answers in writing before you sign a final contract. Some professionals use the proposal with your amendments as the actual contract, others send a short separate form that says something like "as specified in the proposal." Unless you have comparable components from each bidder, you can't really assess competing bids.

The proposal should be very clear about payment and also about cancellation provisions. It is common for caterers to ask for half the money on signing and the second half on the day of the event. Some expect payment at the party in cash or by certified check. Obviously, you need to know this in advance if you are to be prepared.

Some items, such as ice delivery, tend to be C.O.D. Once again, if you are expected to pay, you need to know in advance.

Service charges may or may not be automatically added to the bill. Some hosts prefer to give tips themselves, others find it easier to have this taken care of automatically for them. Whatever your preference, an added 15 to 18 percent for service should not come as a surprise. And you should know whether the service charge includes the waiters or only the kitchen staff. You may think you have tipped the waiters, only to learn at the last minute that you have not.

Read the proposal carefully. It is your best insurance against disappointments and problems. Once you have checked references thoroughly and found prices are comparable, you can relax and trust your instincts about choosing the right professional. In the end, the right person is simply the one who makes you feel the most confident and comfortable. And the better the channels of communication you establish with your caterer or party planner about what you want, the more likely they are to deliver the kind of party you envision. And that means money well spent.

WORKING WITH YOUR PARTY PROFESSIONAL

REMEMBER THAT THE CATERER NEEDS an accurate attendance count to give you a fair price. The proposal should be clear as to whether the caterer requires a minimum number of guests and when your

deadline is for giving a final tally. Most will work with a ballpark figure until three to five days before the event; then they need a final count. It is well worth your while to get on the phone and check with those who have not responded to your invitations so that you do not greatly overestimate your numbers. On the other hand, don't cut corners too closely, since nothing is worse than running out of food. A professional should be able to help you estimate your numbers from his or her past experience with similar groups. Most caterers suggest that it is worthwhile to allow for a few extra people at a large sit-down dinner as a safeguard against last-minute acceptances, just for your peace of mind.

On your part, make a careful list of things you want the caterer or hall to provide, such as sign-in tables, a table to hold favors, or coat-checking facilities, so there is no chance for misunderstandings. Then be sure your list is incorporated into the proposal or contract.

No matter how competent the professional, when it is your party, never assume that the planner or caterer will take care of everything. Party professionals are only human, too, and it is up to you to use the checklists on page 202 to be sure that nothing has been forgotten.

And remember, while professionals can and should make suggestions, in the final analysis, *you* are paying the bills. The ultimate decisions on menu, props, and location are up to you. Once again, the more you learn about these vital party components, the better you will be able to make these decisions with confidence.

An All-Star Production in Hollywood

IT WAS A HOLLYWOOD spectacular that deserved its own Oscar (and actually did win an award for its producer) starring cops and robbers, guys and dolls, Queen Elizabeth and her knights, and a host of break-dancing aliens who descended from the heavens in their own spaceship. Even in Hollywood, where elaborate productions are commonplace, this was a party to remember—and over a year in the making.

Some of the party's fun details: Martian invaders, *above and opposite,* turned out to be breakdancers, and the courtyard of the medieval castle was cleared to reveal a dance floor.

WHO

MINOLTA
CORPORATION
BUSINESS EQUIPMENT
DIVISION

WHAT

AN EVENING OF
DINNER AND DANCING

WHERE

UNIVERSAL STUDIOS,
UNIVERSAL CITY,
CALIFORNIA

WHY

INCENTIVE TRIP FOR
HONOR COUNCIL
DEALERS

For twelve years, Minolta's Business Equipment Division had rewarded dealers who met or exceeded their sales quotas with membership in an Honor Council. This year's council bonus trip for 225 dealers and guests and 91 Minolta staff members included four luxurious entertainment-filled days at the elegant Ritz-Carlton Hotel in Laguna Niguel, California, and a final two days in Los Angeles.

● **2:30 P.M.–7:30 P.M.** When you've wined and dined your guests for six days with the best Southern California has to offer, what do you do for a finale? Party Planners West's ingenious and highly detailed plan began with a "casting call" from Universal Studios. Early Saturday morning, Honor Council members were asked to pick up Screen Actors Guild cards at their hotel. At 2:30 P.M. they boarded buses for Universal Studios, along with some other familiar figures heading for the same casting call—

A bare studio street set, *above,* served as the delightful party backdrop. Although elaborate, the set was far from complete. It was up to a party planner to attend to the details, from putting plants in the window boxes to painting proper signs in the storefront windows, *right.*

Music, *above,* made the street come alive and set guests to dancing; actors dressed as Keystone Kops and gangsters added humor to the scene, *left and opposite.*

While the party planner completed food preparations, guests enjoyed a guided tour of Universal Studios accompanied by actors dressed as Mae West, Groucho Marx, and Jean Harlow, *above and right.* On the backlot set, *opposite,* costumed actors mingled with guests and danced in the street, standing in as "extras" in a 1920s movie extravaganza.

look-alikes for Hollywood greats.

Planner Pat Ryan arranged for a special abbreviated tour of the studio from 3:45 to 5:00 P.M., followed by a screen test for a few unsuspecting candidates for stardom. At 6:00 P.M. a director arrived to hurry the group to a backlot set, where they were to perform as "extras" in a special production. "Eat, drink, dance . . . look like you're having a good time," he told them. These were easy instructions to follow: this street was alive with activity. Vendors at food carts offered tempting hors d'oeuvres cleverly set up as part of the street scene.

● **7:30 P.M.–9:30 P.M.** Promptly at 7:30 P.M., two knights in jousting armor issued a fanfare summoning

To make the street scene even more realistic, signs were created to make it seem as if the foods being served came from the shops behind them, *above and right.*

Carts used to serve up lavish displays of party food were a colorful part of the street scene, *above.*

A fresh oyster and clam bar, *right,* was a fun change from the usual cocktail fare.

SEAFOOD CAFE
FRESH BROOK TROUT
CRAB
FRESH SWORDFISH
FRESH CAPE BLUEFISH

the surprised guests to dinner. When they followed the knights up the hill, they found themselves in the courtyard of the Tower of London, where Queen Elizabeth presided over a medieval banquet.

Once again, the area was bustling with activity, from live animals to period-costumed street people. The banquet buffet offered all the trappings of a medieval groaning board, from pheasant to roast boar. But Ray Henderson of Rococo Caterers believed that, while guests might enjoy looking at foods from the past, they would probably prefer a modern menu. He set up an outdoor kitchen in the back lot for grilled foods. The only thing this sumptuous feast had in common with banquets of old was that many of the foods could be eaten with the hands.

● **9:30 P.M.–11:30 P.M.** Despite the delicious feast, the long week of activity was telling on the tired guests once dinner was over—until

Knights in armor, *opposite,* led the way to the castle scene, *above.* Party planner Pat Ryan provided shrubbery at the gates, long banquet tables with benches spraypainted to match, and had the tents, banners, and throne that were part of the medieval set, *left,* made to order. The serving staff, *below,* in their medieval finery.

Medieval performers and musicians mingled and provided entertainment, while court jesters, *above,* provided laughs. *Opposite:* Most of Rococo's food, something of a legend in the L.A. area, is prepared on-site rather than cooked in advance and reheated; the difference in quality is unmistakable.

Pat's grand finale woke them up again. Rumbling sounds and eerie music came over the loudspeakers, while smoke lights gave the sky an otherworldly glow. Then a spectacular blaze of lights exploded in the sky, revealing the arrival of a "spaceship." It was a vision aglow in multicolored spotlights and twinkling with lights of its own. The *oohs* and *aahs* were audible—as were the cries of delight when a futuristic car came through the gate leading a delegation of break-dancing aliens. The speakers broadcast contagious dance music while klieg lights and cascades of other lights and Mylar from the tower turrets lit up the sky. The aliens grabbed partners among the guests and led them to the floor and the party burst to life all over again. Guests who had been longing to return to the hotel a few minutes earlier suddenly wanted to dance all night.

For a party planner, this kind of extravaganza requires coordinating a variety of talents, much as producing a film does. While Los Angeles offers resources beyond those available in most cities, a top planner must know exactly which ones to tap for the best in every category—which caterer has the

imagination and capability to handle this kind of event, which rental company can come through with deep medieval colors for linens and pewter plates and tankards for the tables. The planner must know who can construct a "spaceship" or create tapes of music appropriate for an alien invasion.

Ryan's preplanning was superb. A Friday night rehearsal made sure that the "spaceship," lights, and music would work the next day without a hitch and that waiters would know how to handle their dry ice–filled dessert trays. As a result of the rehearsal, Pat fine-tuned her production, shortening the mood music tape so the momentum would build more quickly.

Equally impressive was her cool in coping with inevitable last-minute problems, particularly when her staff was spread over three locations. Doing much of the setup a full day ahead of time helped ease the crunch of would-be crises as did a walkie-talkie communication system between locations.

The final party following a lavish incentive trip needs to be a block-buster in order to send everyone home on a high note. One important element in the outstanding success of this particular party was the care Pat Ryan took to see that guests were actively involved, rather than just standing by watching a performance on a movie set. Minolta's guests left knowing that they had been a part of something very special, and with the knowledge that the company valued—and rewarded—its top performers.

Minolta Extravaganza Menu

BY ROCOCO
CATERERS

**STREET
SCENE FOODS**

*Deli-Sausage Cart of Italian
Sausages and Cheeses*

Storefront Oyster Bar

*Vegetable Cart Display of Iced Raw
Vegetables with Dips*

*Storefront Pizza Stand with Choice
of Mozzarella-Tomato-Basil Pizza,
Vegetable Pizza, and
Duck Sausage Pizza*

**MEDIEVAL DINNER
BUFFET**

*Herb-Basted Mesquite-Broiled
Capon and Game Hens*

Coals-Roasted Rack of Lamb

*Roasted Rack of Veal with Wild
Mushroom Sauce*

Poached Salmon with Sorrel Sauce

Cracked Wheat Pilaf

Corn Cobettes

*Mixed Fresh Vegetables with
Lemon Dressing*

DESSERTS IN A CLOUD

*Individual Mixed Pastries
and Chocolates*

The "space ship," *opposite,* hovered directly overhead, held aloft by a crane carefully concealed behind the court-yard, *top.* A trial run the night before made sure that "lift-off" ran smoothly, and an eerie sound-track added to the drama as it loomed in sight. Friendly aliens, *above,* were the ship's cargo.

The Right Space

FINDING A PARTY SPACE used to mean heading for a hotel and inspecting rooms of the right size for your group. There are still times when hotels may offer the most convenient location for entertaining and the only facilities that can accommodate very large numbers. (See page 54 for more hotel pros and cons.) But when you have a choice, interesting spaces inevitably make for more interesting parties.

Chapter 5

The right location, in fact, can *make* a party. It can help ensure more acceptances to your invitations, set a mood, provide an ice-breaking conversational topic, and assure the kind of flow that's needed for a lively and congenial evening.

Finding an unusual space may take a bit of digging, but it's worth the time and effort. In your own city, watch the local papers and magazines for write-ups of unusual party locations and keep them in your party file. Here are other ways to track down party spaces:

- check the library for reference books on party spaces
- contact the parks department and local museums, foundations, and historic homes to ask whether they rent their space for entertaining. Many handsome public buildings now allow parties, which provide them an excellent source of extra revenue
- if members of your company belong to private clubs or serve on the boards of cultural institutions,

they may be able to reserve space for you in places that are not available to the general public.

At home or away, as I mentioned in Chapter 3, a well-connected party planner or caterer is frequently the best source of all when it comes to finding special locations. Many take pride in coming up with exclusive spaces.

FINDING A PERFECT FIT

WHEN YOU LOOK AT SPACES, THE first requirement is a practical one —a room that will accommodate the number of people you expect to entertain. A room that is too large creates an uncomfortable empty feeling, whereas overcrowding can make a party space hot, noisy, smoky, and generally unpleasant. When possible, try to see the room set up for a crowd the size of your party so that you can judge the atmosphere and space.

There is nothing to be done when a space is too small, but if you fall in love with a room that seems too big, you can sometimes make it work by sectioning the space into more manageable areas with dividers.

A spacious loft was the natural setting for a publication party for Suzanne Slesin and Stafford Cliff's *International Book of Lofts*, but I was concerned that it might be too large for the number of guests we planned on. We solved the problem

Be sure the space you choose is easily accessible by car, taxi, or public transportation, and don't forget to consider parking logistics.

with a giant screen that divided the room into two spaces. We projected photographs on both sides of the screen and the guests did not seem lost in the smaller spaces on either side of the screen.

Sometimes a large open space that seems cavernous when empty can be transformed into a wonderful party setting. Companies in New York often rent the enormous Seventh Regiment Armory building, then make the space more

intimate with decorations or by constructing a tent inside. This vast space has been turned into a winter wonderland with 350 evergreen trees, tons of "snow," and Santa on a sleigh as well as into a Moroccan bazaar for 1,100, complete with Berber tribesmen and live camels. You could do the same with a gymnasium or sports arena. Beware, however, of renting a too-large space for too few people—it always has a dampening effect.

SIZING UP PARTY SPACE

THE BEST PARTY SPACES LEND THEM-selves to easy mingling. A static party is a boring party. Placement of the food, drinks, music, and other attractions should keep guests moving—and there should be plenty of room to move comfortably. Walk through potential spaces to envision the party flow. If the site itself doesn't provide different levels or other easy dividing elements to keep people circulating, can you create them? If not, better look for another space. Here are points to check:

- can bars and food stations be placed in different areas to encourage movement?
- at sit-down dinners, will there be ample room for sign-ins and getting table assignments? For cocktails before the meal? For serving space between tables? Is there room for a dessert buffet to get guests mingling?
- if you plan food stations, is there enough floor space for people to circulate easily from one to another?
- is there room for enough bars and buffet tables to avoid crowding?
- will there be enough elbow room for people passing through the buffet lines?
- with buffet service, is there space for a few tables for those who prefer to eat sitting down?
- for cocktail parties, is there space for a few tables where guests can put down empty glasses? (You needn't, however, plan extra space for seating areas at a cocktail party. Too many tables and chairs tend to divide the group—people gravitate toward their friends and do not mingle.)
- if you are having music, will there be space where guests can watch the musicians? Room for a dance floor?
- at a large party, using different kinds of music in different areas draws people from one to another. Will your site allow this?
- is there space for a coat check area that does not interfere with the flow of guests at the party?
- are restrooms easily accessible to the space and sufficient in number?

● **THE RIGHT IMAGE.** By the time you begin looking at locations, you will have decided just what kind of mood you hope to create—formal or funky, elegant or easygoing—and the space should fit that mood. Bear in mind that part of your purpose is to make the party reflect and reinforce the image your organization wants to project. A recent party demonstrated how space can project the right mood and image. A watch manufacturer whose advertising positions it as a pacesetter in technology needed a special space for entertaining buyers during a jewelry industry meeting and show in New York. The company chose a dance club called The Saint, which offers the very latest in high-tech lighting, an actual replica of the sophisticated machinery used in the Hayden Planetarium. The mood was upbeat, the message was high tech. And the lighting made this party stand out in the memory of those who would be attending many affairs given by competing companies. The party became a living extension of the company's marketing image.

A bank or major corporation might prefer a more dignified image. That is often satisfied by holding a function in a local historic building or museum, helping to establish the company as a patron of the arts as well as an institution of good taste. The Bank of New York and the investment house of Morgan Stanley are among many companies that have entertained in the impressive spaces of the New York Public Library. New York's Whitney Museum has been used by DuPont for a new-product launch and by First Boston Bank for a dinner celebrating the

A Landmark Space

A New York City convention can be a challenge for party-givers. The usual competition for guests by rival companies is increased by the many lures of the city itself.

The Micrographic Division of Fuji Photo Film U.S.A. solved that problem neatly by coming up with a landmark location for their cocktail buffet. Federal Hall, the first capitol of the United States, is a National Historic Site in the heart of New York's Wall Street area, a location many New York visitors would like to see but find hard to fit into a busy convention schedule. The turnout was tremendous, even on a rainy evening.

This was also a party perfectly planned for crowd flow. A big charcuterie table in the center of the great domed rotunda and a series of food stations with chefs in action around the perimeter enticed guests to keep moving from one place to the next.

Mammoth columns and a soaring, domed rotunda, *above and opposite,* make Federal Hall an impressive party space with historic resonance.

Off to Sea

Wherever you find water, sunsets, and city lights, going to sea is a winning way to entertain—but with certain cautions. Guests can't "drop in" on a boat party. Cruises are a poor choice for the media or other busy people, many of whom will not accept boat invitations because they can't afford to be confined for the duration of the party.

Caterers also report that far more liquor is consumed at sea than on land because guests who might otherwise have departed after a drink or two are trapped and continue drinking. And some people do find the confinement uncomfortable.

However, there is no denying the lure of the sea, and boat parties can provide wonderful memories in a new city. So don't rule them out; just be smart and follow these rules:

- *choose short cruises of no more than two hours*
- *consider a party on a boat docked in the harbor, where there is nautical atmosphere as well as the opportunity for guests to go ashore when they are ready. (If the boat will be docked, be sure the invitation makes that clear.)*
- *try using a boat as transportation—hire a ferry, for example, to transport guests to a wonderful riverside restaurant*
- *have plenty of nonalcoholic beverages on board*
- *have some seasick medication on board if you cruise, just in case.*

closing of a deal. One drug manufacturer attracted a good crowd to a party at the Massachusetts Historical Society that offered the chance to visit an elegant Back Bay mansion; John Hancock's chair and Daniel Webster's desk made for interesting conversation-starters.

Depending on the city, museum rentals can range anywhere from $500 to the whopping $250,000 contribution New York's Metropolitan Museum of Art asks, entitling corporate donors to use the museum spaces for entertaining. While the cost of such locations may be high, rental fees often are considered charitable donations and may be partially tax deductible.

Events in public spaces can fit a variety of needs. A New York City law firm used the basement-level entry court of the Whitney Museum for a barbecue cookout with a Western band, a way to entertain its summer interns in a prestigious location without the stiff formality of a sit-down dinner. A mid-Atlantic automobile dealer invited its employees and their families to enjoy an evening at the Philadelphia Zoo, where typical Philly foods were served by costumed street vendors. In Chicago, party planner Mary Ann Josh helped a commodities trading firm plan an original Oriental dinner menu that made for a particularly festive evening in the Field Museum.

● **MORE POSSIBILITIES.** Other, less obvious public spaces can be wonderful party sites as well. A large Midwestern food manufacturer rented the MetroDome in Minneapolis for a company outing that included a good-natured mini-Olympics competition. City parks

A tent can make nearly any public space into a party space. Be sure the one you choose has side flaps in case of bad weather (and to obscure unsightly equipment and electrical wiring if necessary).

often have buildings that offer party spaces in sylvan surroundings, and many companies set up gala tents for functions in special outdoor settings such as Independence Park in Philadelphia or the Mall in Washington, D.C. One of Miami's most eagerly anticipated benefits is the Flamingo Ball, held each year at the Hialeah Racetrack.

Art galleries are popular party sites in many cities. Restored railroad stations can make attractive settings for large events and so can the stage or the lobby of an elegant theater or period movie house. Airplane hangars, wine cellars, private yachts, even the *Q.E. II* can be

rented for a party. And a movie or TV sound stage is a blank canvas, waiting to be transformed into any backdrop your imagination can conjure up.

When you approach places that are not normally used for entertaining, be clear on who is responsible for insurance and what assistance will be provided for coat checking, parking, security, rest rooms, and kitchen facilities, as well as what restrictions there may be on what may be brought into the building and what kind of cleanup you must provide. It should be established in advance just what you can expect to find when you arrive and how you are expected to leave things when you depart after the event.

Also remember that many popular restaurants and "in" discos will rent out for parties on a night when they are normally closed to the public or provide a separate room for parties. Restaurants where reservations are hard to come by draw a good turnout for parties.

By all means, don't overlook the possibility of holding your event in a private residence. Every city has a roster of lovely private homes that can be rented for entertaining, from the "Dallas" mansion in Los Angeles to Southern plantations in Atlanta or stunning artists' lofts in New York City's SoHo district. And if someone in your company has an exceptional home, it may be the warmest setting of all.

When you can hold a party in a private home or club that is not ordinarily open to the public, your party offers a special attraction, a draw that can be especially important at a convention where companies compete to entertain the same people. For the same reason, it can be beneficial to entertain in a desirable area of the city that people might want to visit during a busy convention.

PRACTICAL PROBLEMS

PROPER SIZE, MOOD, AND ORIGINALITY are among the first considerations, but there are several other factors to consider when you look over party spaces.

One important factor is work space for the caterers. Can they present the kind of food you want with the kitchen facilities available? A competent caterer can do wonders with portable ovens or a cook tent almost anywhere, but your

menu may have to change if cooking facilities on the premises are not adequate for fancy preparation. (As mentioned earlier, it is very reassuring to choose a caterer who has worked in the space before.)

Another matter to check is access to the service entries and elevators where food and rentals are delivered and how far things must be carried from the elevator to the party site. In New York City, some busy buildings can keep a caterer waiting as long as two hours to get into the freight elevator. Imagine what that would do to an ice carving planned as the centerpiece for your buffet!

It is also a good idea to inquire whether the building will provide storage space for rentals before and after the party. Some companies charge extra if deliveries and pickups must be made on the same day.

Finding Party Places in a New City

Finding unique party space in an unfamiliar city presents a special challenge. Here are a few tips on how to proceed:

- *begin with the Convention and Visitors Bureau. Many large cities now publish convention guides that include both names of caterers and ideas for unusual entertaining locations. (You might check this guide for your own city also—it may offer some new discoveries.)*
- *mayors' offices are often a good source of ideas*
- *local food and life-style editors and city magazines are reliable sources of information.*

Getting There Is Part of the Party

If you use buses to transport party guests to an outlying location, don't forget that the trip is setting the mood for your event. Here are precautions to take to ensure that your guests' first impression of the event awaiting them will be a favorable one:

- *have someone to greet guests personally as they get on and off the bus*
- *offer refreshments during the ride, if possible*
- *add an unexpected twist—like the movie star look-alikes at left, or a fortune-teller or palm-reader*
- *provide music—either a live musician or taped selections*
- *think about having someone take Polaroid pictures of guests as they board and hand them out during the trip*
- *give out a clever favor—a travel guide or song sheets that might encourage singing on the way*

Playful look-alikes from Hollywood's heyday sat with passengers and livened up the trip to Universal Studios for Minolta's guests, *above*. And don't feel a bus is out of the question just be-cause your event is black tie, *right*. Offering your passengers cham-pagne and having a musician on board will make the ride less tedious and set an elegant tone for the evening ahead.

As you look around, you'll want to check on other practicalities:

- are there convenient rest rooms and coat check areas?
- what are the light sources?
- is the elevator adequate to bring your guests up and down without too much waiting?
- are there enough electrical outlets for any needed additional light-ing? Can the circuits carry the extra load?
- are cabs and/or parking facilities available nearby?

Some problems of this kind can be worked out with advance plan-ning, but if a site presents too many problems, you may be better off at another location.

● **GETTING TO THE PARTY.** Party trans-portation is a major consideration. Obviously, it is easier to get to centrally located facilities, but sometimes the most unique and desirable sites are outside of the city or in outlying neighborhoods. Price the cost of chartering buses or trolleys and add that to the rental cost for an overall figure before you make a final decision. The cost of a bus may be small compared to the excitement an unusual space can generate.

If you do choose an out-of-the-way location, be sure to include clear directions and a map with your invitation. If transportation is being offered, be very specific about where it will leave from and when. And don't forget to think about how your guests will get back home late at night. You may have to arrange for buses once again, or make special arrangements with a taxi company to have cars on hand. (This may turn out to be more of a headache than it appears. We had made arrangements for cabs to pick up guests leaving a book publication party in San Francisco, but the taxis did not show up on time, leaving important clients standing outside. It would have been wiser to hire a trolley or a bus.)

If you decide on a party in a remote place or on a boat, remember that guests can't leave when they want. That can be a disadvantage unless you are Malcolm Forbes and have a helicopter standing by. Provide a list of phone numbers of nearby taxi services in case guests want to leave before the scheduled departure time.

● OTHER CONSIDERATIONS. When you are considering an outdoor location, look for shelter, lighting, and portable heating facilities in case of rain or cold weather. Once again, these can be brought in, but if you are comparing two or three sites, you may prefer the one that re-

quires the least extra preparation.

If you have a theme party with scenery in mind, you are ahead of the game if your planner has done similar events successfully in the space you are considering and is familiar with the facilities. It may also be a good idea to call in a lighting consultant to look things over before you make a final decision. For a large theme party, it is important to remember that the location is really only a backdrop. Flowers, lighting, and props can completely change any room.

When you negotiate a contract for your party space, be sure you are allotting enough time for setting up beforehand and for cleaning up afterwards. Three hours is a bare minimum for setting up comfortably and you will need at least two hours after the party for cleanup. You may be better off hiring the space for a full day rather than risk having to pay overtime charges.

The right space will become a backdrop that allows you to create party magic. And if you choose well, the space will create a bit of magic on its own.

Potential Party Spaces

- *Museums*
- *Elegant theaters*
- *Period movie houses*
- *Airport hangars*
- *Ferryboats*
- *Yachts*
- *Trolley cars*
- *Warehouses*
- *Art galleries*
- *City parks*
- *Racetracks*
- *Zoos*
- *Railroad stations*
- *Private mansions*
- *Historic houses*
- *Sports arenas*
- *Shopping center atriums*
- *Office building lobbies*
- *Gardens*
- *City plazas*
- *Homes of company executives*

At Home with House Beautiful

MARCIA MILLER has the kind of home that could easily be featured in her own magazine, an apartment with a fascinating history and location plus enormous warmth. It was the perfect location when Marcia and her staff decided to revive the idea of the salon, a small, elite gathering of interesting people and lively conversation. In this case, all of the guests were to be connected with the magazine.

WHO

HOUSE BEAUTIFUL MAGAZINE

WHAT

COCKTAIL SALON

WHERE

HOME OF *HB* PUBLISHER, MARCIA MILLER

WHY

ENTERTAIN ADVERTISERS AND CONTRIBUTORS

This salon would serve a special business purpose. *House Beautiful* has long been known as a classically elegant magazine, but its content has been changing to keep up with contemporary life-styles. How does a company get advertisers to notice that it is changing? Entertaining can play a key role, particularly if you have an intimate setting that provides a chance to really talk to people who matter about what is happening behind the scenes.

The series of monthly salons was designed to bring together key advertisers and opinion makers with the top designers and manufacturers whose work was featured in the current issue. The fact that these top names were associated with the publication was a statement on its

Noted decorator
Mario Buatta, *above,*
was guest of honor
at this gathering. His
contribution to the
current issue of
House Beautiful was
a room in his trade-
mark English
chintzes. The inti-
mate size of the
gathering and the
hospitable ambience
of a private home
created an atmo-
sphere conducive to
the kind of network-
ing the salon was
meant to promote,
right.

own. The flowers and food would
be models of modern entertaining,
subtly mirroring the magazine's
new editorial direction.

To encourage easy conversation
at each gathering, the guest list was
limited to fifty and carefully planned
to allow for a good mix of old and
new acquaintances, people with
enough professional interests in
common to make for the exchange
of ideas that had distinguished the
old salons.

The sense of intimacy carried
through when Marcia presented the
honorees to her other guests. It was
less the introduction of celebrities
than sharing treasured friends with
other special acquaintances.

This was a perfect demonstration
of why party size should be determined by your goals. The most
lavish large party would never have
provided the personal warmth or
the opportunity for individual conversations that these evenings
presented. The *House Beautiful* staff
was able to single out the people
they most wanted to reach and
make them feel special. They built
both fresh awareness and goodwill
for the magazine.

The gentle music of a
harp, *opposite,* pro-
vided a lovely,
nonintrusive back-
ground that allowed
people to converse
freely.

House Beautiful Menu
BY PLUMS CATERING

Fresh Vegetable Crudité Basket

Endive with Herbed Chèvre

*Haricots Verts Wrapped with
Smoked Mozzarella and Prosciutto*

*Filet Rolled Around Broiled
Scallions with Teriyaki Sauce*

Cold Poached Lobster

Sesame Chicken on a Skewer

*Smoked Norwegian Salmon on
Black Bread with Lemon and
Pear Butter Spread*

*Roast Lamb Kebabs with Red and
Yellow Bell Peppers*

*White Chocolate
Champagne Truffles*

*Long-Stemmed
Chocolate-Dipped Strawberries*

A small party allows for elegant touches that might not be affordable with larger numbers, such as smoked salmon and sliced filet of beef, *opposite.* Lavish bouquets graced every room.

Caterer Richard de Asis of Plums arranged inventive hors d'oeuvres on oversized lacquered black trays with the precision of a Japanese print. The design was maintained by frequent refills from the kitchen, *right,* another little luxury that only works effectively with a smaller group. The hostess's own lace cloth, *above,* was used on the table.

Along with a copy of the June issue of *House Beautiful,* guests were given a stylish white umbrella with the magazine's logo colorfully bordering the edges. No sooner had they descended to the street than the rain finally came, but the guests left with their new umbrellas —and their spirits— high, *opposite.*

Above, right, and far right: A home setting always gives a party special warmth. Marcia Miller's sixthfloor apartment is filled with architectural details—a lovely courtyard entrance, an interior by Stanford White, glorious paneling, plasterwork, and antique stained-glass insets in the windows, to delight guests.

Even the flowers carry out the more personal feeling of business entertaining at home. Small bouquets of roses and wildflowers by Twigs

Florist were placed throughout the apartment, picking up the needlepointed motif on the sofa pillows, *above.*

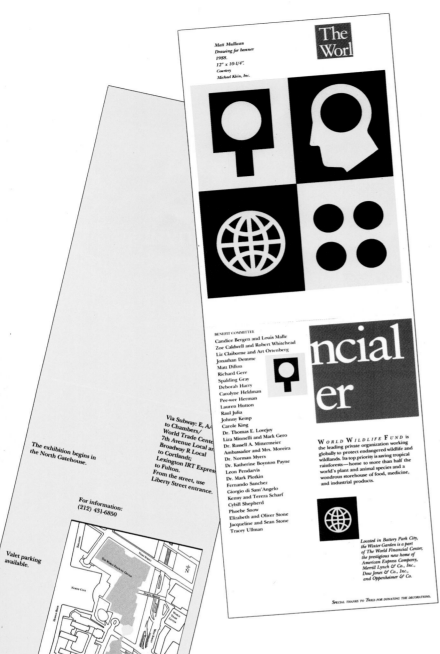

Matt Mullican
Drawing for banner
1988.
12" x 10-1/4".
Courtesy
Michael Klein, Inc.

The Worl

ncial
er

BENEFIT COMMITTEE
Candice Bergen and Louis Malle
Zoe Caldwell and Robert Whitehead
Liz Claiborne and Art Ortenberg
Jonathan Demme
Matt Dillon
Richard Gere
Spalding Gray
Deborah Harry
Carolyne Heldman
Pee-wee Herman
Lauren Hutton
Raul Julia
Johnny Kemp
Carole King
Dr. Thomas E. Lovejoy
Lira Minnelli and Mark Gero
Dr. Russell A. Mittermeier
Ambassador and Mrs. Moreira
Dr. Norman Myers
Dr. Katherine Boynton Payne
Leon Pendarvis
Dr. Mark Plotkin
Fernando Sanchez
Giorgio di Sant'Angelo
Kenny and Tereza Scharf
Cybill Shepherd
Phoebe Snow
Elizabeth and Oliver Stone
Jacqueline and Sean Stone
Tracey Ullman

WORLD WILDLIFE FUND is
the leading private organization working
globally to protect endangered wildlife and
wildlands. Its top priority is saving tropical
rainforests—home to more than half the
world's plant and animal species and a
wondrous storehouse of food, medicine,
and industrial products.

Via Subway: E, AA
to Chambers/
World Trade Center
7th Avenue Local and
Broadway R Local
to Cortlandt;
Lexington IRT Express
to Fulton.
From the street, use
Liberty Street entrance.

The exhibition begins in
the North Gatehouse.

For information:
(212) 431-6850

Valet parking
available.

Located in Battery Park City,
the Winter Garden is a part
of The World Financial Center,
the prestigious new home of
American Express Company,
Merrill Lynch & Co., Inc.,
Dow Jones & Co., Inc.,
and Oppenheimer & Co.

SPECIAL THANKS TO TWIGS FOR DONATING THE DECORATIONS.

Clear, concise directions are an essential part of the invitation when the locale of your event is unfamiliar. Include a diagram or map wherever possible.

sentation at the event, the invitation should make this clear.

The invitation should also be clear about what kind of food will be served. The menu for a breakfast, lunch, or high tea is taken for granted, but evening parties can offer a variety of fare. "Cocktails" implies light passed food; "cocktail buffet" usually means a more lavish menu, but still less than a full dinner. Both usually begin between 5:30 and 6:00 P.M., right after work, and last until about 8:00 P.M.

A buffet supper indicates that a

full meal will be served, though a less formal one than a sit-down dinner. Like a dinner, it usually starts at 7:30 or 8:00 P.M. and may be preceded by cocktails. If you are planning a late-night party, be clear if only desserts are planned or if there will be a midnight supper. If there will be dancing, the invitation should say so.

If the party location is difficult to find, enclosing a map is very helpful. If there are any special instructions about transportation or parking, these should be included as well.

DESIGNING THE LOOK OF YOUR INVITATION

THE CLASSIC FORMAL INVITATION IS always engraved in black ink on white or ecru and is usually a double-fold card. But unless the occasion or the company's image calls for such formality, innovative designs that set the mood and whet the appetite for the event may do

Ms JoAnn Barwick
House Beautiful

Distinguished guests include:
Ms Ann A...
Ms A...

Marcia Miller & JoAnn Barwick
request the pleasure of
Ms Jo Ann Barwick
for an Evening Salon
honoring
Mr Mario Buatta
on
Wednesday, June 3, 1987
6:00 to 8:00 pm
at the home of Marcia Miller
455 E. 51st Street, Apt. 6A
RSVP 903-5118

Matt Mullican
Drawing for banner
1988.
12" x 10-1/4".
Courtesy
Michael Klein, Inc.

The Worl

BENEFIT COMMITTEE
Candice Bergen and Louis Malle
Zoe Caldwell and Robert Whitehead
Liz Claiborne and Art Ortenberg
Jonathan Demme
Matt Dillon
Richard Gere
Spalding Gray
Deborah Harry
Carolyne Heldman
Pee-wee Herman
Lauren Hutton
Raul Julia
Johnny Kemp
Carole King
Dr. Thomas E. Lovejoy
Liza Minnelli and Mark Gero
Dr. Russell A. Mittermeier
Ambassador and Mrs. Moreira
Dr. Norman Myers
Dr. Katherine Boynton Payne
Leon Pendarvis
Dr. Mark Plotkin
Fernando Sanchez
Giorgio di Sant'Angelo
Kenny and Tereza Scharf
Cybill Shepherd
Phoebe Snow
Elizabeth and Oliver Stone
Jacqueline and Sean Stone
Tracey Ullman

ncial
er

WORLD WILDLIFE FUND is
the leading private organization working
globally to protect endangered wildlife and
wildlands. Its top priority is saving tropical
rainforests—home to more than half the
world's plant and animal species and a
wondrous storehouse of food, medicine,
and industrial products.

Located in Battery Park City,
the Winter Garden is a part
of The World Financial Center,
the prestigious new home of
American Express Company,
Merrill Lynch & Co., Inc.,
Dow Jones & Co., Inc.,
and Oppenheimer & Co.

SPECIAL THANKS TO TBWG FOR DONATING THE DECORATIONS.

Via Subway: E, AA
to Chambers/
World Trade Cente
7th Avenue Local an
Broadway R Local
to Cortlandt;
Lexington IRT Express
to Fulton.
From the street, use
Liberty Street entrance.

The exhibition begins in
the North Gatehouse.

For information:
(212) 431-6850

Valet parking
available.

Clear, concise directions are an essential part of the invitation when the locale of your event is unfamiliar. Include a diagram or map wherever possible.

sentation at the event, the invitation should make this clear.

The invitation should also be clear about what kind of food will be served. The menu for a breakfast, lunch, or high tea is taken for granted, but evening parties can offer a variety of fare. "Cocktails" implies light passed food; "cocktail buffet" usually means a more lavish menu, but still less than a full dinner. Both usually begin between 5:30 and 6:00 P.M., right after work, and last until about 8:00 P.M.

A buffet supper indicates that a full meal will be served, though a less formal one than a sit-down dinner. Like a dinner, it usually starts at 7:30 or 8:00 P.M. and may be preceded by cocktails. If you are planning a late-night party, be clear if only desserts are planned or if there will be a midnight supper. If there will be dancing, the invitation should say so.

If the party location is difficult to find, enclosing a map is very helpful. If there are any special instructions about transportation or parking, these should be included as well.

DESIGNING THE LOOK OF YOUR INVITATION

THE CLASSIC FORMAL INVITATION IS always engraved in black ink on white or ecru and is usually a double-fold card. But unless the occasion or the company's image calls for such formality, innovative designs that set the mood and whet the appetite for the event may do the job better. You want your invitation to stand out among the many that come through the mail. Interesting shapes, appealing colors, and a bit of humor help set the stage for a gala event—but always, of course, within the bounds of good taste.

In many large cities you can find designers who specialize in creating innovative invitations. Party planners also often employ experienced invitation designers. Then too, someone in your company's art department may be able to help. To commission an artist to do an original design may cost anywhere from $100 to $750, but if that expenditure is instrumental in prompting key people to accept the invitation, it can be money well spent.

For very personal business entertaining, such as entertaining at home, a short handwritten note is sometimes the most gracious way to extend an invitation. All invitations should be hand addressed—and by someone with good, legible handwriting. Calligraphy is one attractive way to address special invitations, but may cost as much as $2 per envelope.

The quality of paper and printing has a lot to do with the overall appearance of an invitation, and you should go with the best your budget will allow. There are many types of card stock to choose from in a variety of colors and textures. See samples of the options offered by two or three different printers before you make your choice. One consideration to remember if you are working within a budget is the weight of the paper; you may want to stay with a weight requiring only a single stamp. Be sure to check this with the printer.

Invitation Fundamentals

Basic information on the invitation should include the following:
- *Who is giving the party*
- *Company name; Any individuals*
- *Purpose of the party*
- *Guest of honor*
- *Date and time(s)*
- *Place of party*
- *Type of food to be served*
- *RSVP information*
- *Dress to be worn*
- *Is card required for admittance*
- *Does card admit one or two*
- *Any necessary travel data*

Specify whether a reply (RSVP) is required, or whether "Regrets only" will be sufficient. Generally, the more food you plan to serve, the more important it is to have an accurate count of how many guests to expect. For this reason, formal dinners usually include a stamped return card for RSVPs.

Invitations That Get Results

Wordings like these on an invitation are more likely to get a response from invitees:
- *RSVP essential.*
- *RSVP by (date) _____.*
- *RSVP to _____ by _____.*

Your invitation should let guests know whether they may bring a guest by stating, "Ms. Jane Smith and guest are invited" or "This invitation admits two."

If you want to limit the number of guests (as well as confer a note of exclusivity), here are some ways to do it politely:
- *"This invitation admits one only."*
- *"Only those on the door list will be admitted."*

To discourage gate crashers, note, "Please present this invitation at the door." Add "This invitation is nontransferable" to ensure that the executive you hope to attract doesn't hand the invitation over to an aide. "Nontransferable" implies an exclusive group and may encourage top brass to attend.

As I've mentioned, compiling the guest list for invitations for a large event should be a joint effort involving many areas of the company, and the invitation should have the approval of important company officials as well.

TIMING

FOUR WEEKS BEFORE THE EVENT IS the usual time to send out invitations, but three months ahead is none too soon to begin to interview printers, look at samples of paper and print styles, get estimates, and place a printing order. I usually like to get three estimates before I decide on a new printer. Once you have worked happily with a firm, you can relax and continue with them.

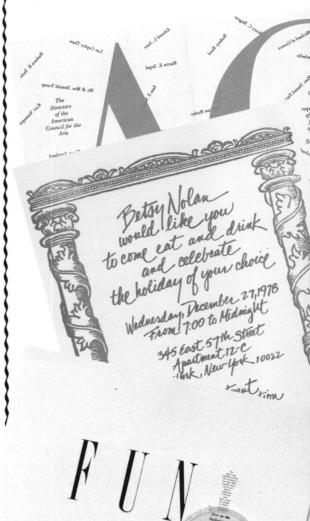

If you are having a special design created, you may need to begin even earlier to find an artist whose work you like. If there is no one on staff, you can usually get suggestions from printers or from advertising or public relations firms that work with artists.

Be certain to allow time to look at a printer's proof before the invi-

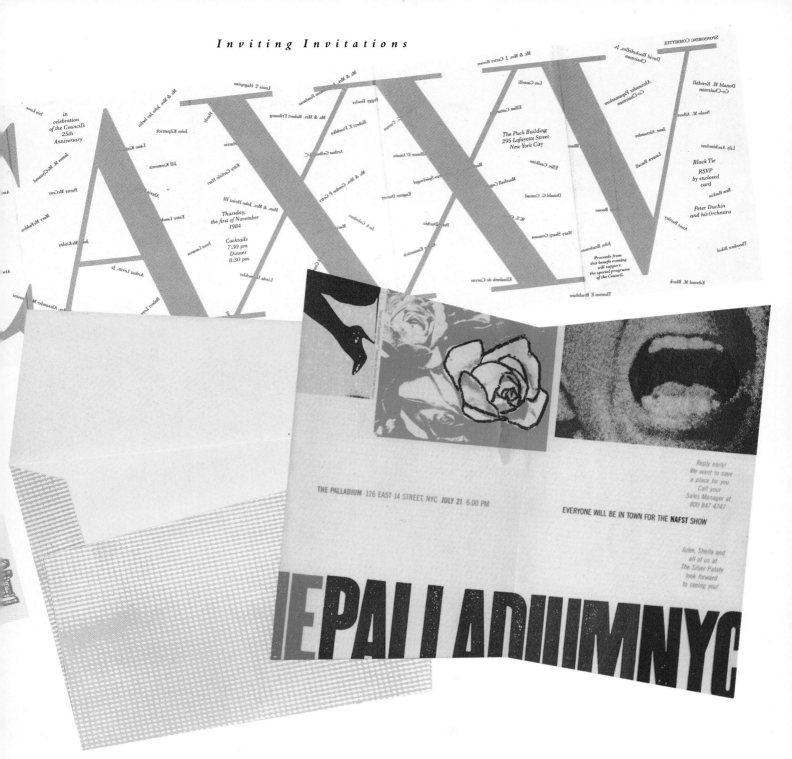

tations are printed. The time to catch spelling errors and mistakes is *before* the presses roll.

And leave ample time for hand addressing, especially if you decide to use calligraphy.

When you are planning an important event, you may want to send out invitations several months ahead and follow up with a re-minder card, or send a preview announcement card telling people to save the date. (See the text of the notice sent by the New Museum alerting members to reserve the date of their tenth-anniversary celebration, *opposite*.)

The checklist on page 204 will help you keep track of your invitations from idea to acceptance.

Invitations should grab your guests' attention and set the tone of the event—whether formal, intimate, outrageous, or grand.

A Grant Park Gala in Chicago

WHEN IS AN INVITATION more than an invitation? When it does double-duty as a concert poster! William Blair & Company was able to accomplish two important goals by combining sponsorship of a public concert with a gala pre-concert dinner for its own staff. It was able to delight employees with an innovative setting and event and enhance the company's image in the community at the same time.

WHO

WILLIAM BLAIR
& COMPANY,
INVESTMENT BANKERS

WHAT

COCKTAILS AND
DINNER, FOLLOWED BY
OPEN-AIR CONCERT

WHERE

GRANT PARK, CHICAGO

WHY

EMPLOYEE
APPRECIATION

Chicago's Grant Park concerts are a summer tradition, a season of more than three dozen free musical events, ranging from pop to classical, and featuring talented young musicians as well as name performers. Because it is a party planner's job to be plugged in to what is happening in her city, Mary Ann Josh of Events Alive knew that the concerts were in need of new corporate sponsorship. She also knew that sponsors have the option of erecting a party tent in the park, a perfect answer to Blair's request for something out of the ordinary for their employee party.

That's how, on a warm August evening, some two hundred members of the William Blair staff found themselves dining in a shimmery white tent in the middle of

With the mercury unexpectedly in the 90s, the caterer changed the hot menu he had planned to one better suited to the weather, changing the warm beurre blanc sauce to a cold tarragon mayonnaise that could be added to plates in the makeshift kitchen, *above,* at the last moment. A concert poster, also the party invitation, *right,* showed guests the way. Handsome presentation of food is one of Chicago Caterer's strengths, from the serving tables designed to fit around tent poles, *opposite,* to their trademark baskets of herbed bread sticks.

the city. During dinner, they were warmly thanked by the company for their contributions to its success. Afterwards, they were ushered to VIP seats for the concert. No valued clients could have been entertained with more flair or care than the William Blair staff enjoyed that night.

Entertaining in an open public space is pleasant in summer, but the logistics are complicated and may add extras to the party bud-

get. Events Alive had to obtain permits from the Chicago Parks Department and meet its requirements. In this case, the firm was asked to produce an insurance certificate for half a million dollars and use union electricians for the lighting. The department, in return, donated hedges and ficus plants from its Lincoln Park conservatory to form a handsome walkway into the party area. Security is also a necessity in a park. Around-the-clock guards were necessary from the time the tent went up the day before the party until the last stake was removed.

Weather is always a concern outdoors. Events Alive covered all the possibilities. Umbrellas were on tap and the tent sides could be lowered in case of rain or chill. And tall fans were in place in case of heat. The only glitch all day came when the tent company left the flaps down, making it uncomfortable for those who were setting up on a sultry summer day. A phone call brought them back to remedy the

A canopied walkway of greenery, *above*, provided a graceful transition from the open park to the party space, and offered protection in case of rain. At a dinner party, music must help maintain the spirit of the party without overwhelming conversation. The jazz combo with violinist, *below*, worked perfectly. Employees were honored guests with front-row seats for the concert, *opposite*, while fellow Chicagoans enjoyed picnic suppers al fresco.

problem, but the fans proved a lifesaver in the meantime.

No effort was spared to make this evening stand out. A generator was rented to power the soft theatrical lights that bounced off the tent ceiling, giving the scene an atmospheric glow. Tablecloths were made to order in a floral print to complement the pinks, peaches, and mauves of the flower arrangements. The party planners even alerted the evening's entertainer, jazz violinist Susie Hansen, so that her band could come dressed to match the color scheme. Nor did

they forget little touches like pretty soap and fresh towels to brighten the public bathrooms.

To ensure that employees would get home safely after the party, the cocktail hour was limited and only wine was served during the meal. The concert following dinner was over by 10:00 P.M., in time to get everyone home early. The company decided against reconvening at the tent for dessert following the concert, realizing that most people faced a long drive and would prefer to get home.

Company parties are an important way for management to tell employees they are valued and should never seem simply an obligation that must be met. What better way to show your staff you think they are special than to fête them in style with the whole city watching? Throughout this dinner, concertgoers approached the tent to ask about the lucky VIPs inside.

Don't feel restricted to solid-colored napkins and tablecloths. This party designer found floral patterned tablecloths and crisp pink napkins that added to the summery feeling of the tent, *above*, and edible flowers decorate herbed bread rounds, *left*. Virginia Wolff's stunning wildflower centerpieces, *opposite*, succeeded brilliantly in adding drama without obstructing sightlines.

Grant Park Gala Menu

BY JIM GUTH, CHICAGO CATERERS

HORS D'OEUVRES BUFFET

Selection of Cheeses and Fresh Fruits, Assorted Wafers and Crackers

Avocado-Caviar Pie

Mascarpone Torte

Crudité Basket

PASSED HORS D'OEUVRES

Smoked Beef Tenderloin Skewers with Horseradish Sauce

Dill Crêpes with Crème Fraîche and Caviar

Grapes Rolled in Cream Cheese and Chopped Pistachio Nuts

Snow Peas with Herbed Cheese

Chinese Pearl Balls

Vegetable Tempura with Ginger Apricot Sauce

DINNER

Bay Scallops with Pea Pods, Watercress, and Boston Lettuce and Sesame Seed Vinaigrette

Old-Fashioned Stuffed Chicken Breasts with Chèvre, Spinach, Wild Mushrooms, and Herb Stuffing and Tarragon Mayonnaise

Julienned Yellow Peppers and Italian Parsley

Rice Pilaf with Raisins, Almonds, and Apricots

Cold Asparagus Spears with Tomato Concassé

Baskets of Assorted Homemade Breadsticks

Fresh Berry Compote with Vanilla Ice Cream

Party Wining and Dining

NOT SO LONG AGO, business party menus were totally predictable. A cocktail party meant an uninspired selection of cheese and crackers and an open bar; luncheon or dinner meant broiled chicken or roast beef. The quality of the food was usually just as predictable—bland and mediocre. Rarely was imagination put into the planning of such menus, and the end result was usually a room full of disgruntled guests.

Chapter

Then along came creative caterers like Glorious Foods and Martha Stewart and suddenly catered food became exciting, both in its preparation and presentation. Today's top caterers can compete successfully with the variety and quality of a fine restaurant's fare. Many pride themselves on their innovative menus. You can and should expect much better than mediocre food from your caterer.

TYPES OF MENUS

MOST PARTY MENUS FALL INTO SET categories, each with certain advantages and disadvantages. You will want to consider which type of entertaining best meets your goals.

Cocktail parties allow you to entertain the most people for the least money, but they are also the least personal type of entertaining. A seated luncheon or dinner is the most elegant way to entertain, but

is also the most expensive. Cocktail buffets and buffet dinners are a compromise, a way to entertain larger numbers graciously but at more moderate cost; they are understandably popular choices.

Most caterers will have standard menus for each of these options, as well as suggestions for breakfast, tea, dessert parties, and other types of entertaining.

Before making a final decision on your caterer, you will have checked references thoroughly and preferably sampled the firm's work. Now it is up to you to get the most from them in planning and serving your own party menu. A caterer needs a sense of your own tastes in order to advise you and please you. Try to convey the type of guests you expect, what part of the country they come from, and the atmosphere you hope to create. Caterers will take their cue from you if you advise that you want an innovative menu or that you prefer something more conservative. Your own wishes may change from party to party according to the guests and the location.

Be very careful about choosing an avant-garde menu that shows off the latest food trends unless you know your guests will appreciate

it. Even a trendy restaurant offers a few less adventurous choices for the timid. At a party, you must please a lot of tastes and often guests ranging in age from twenty-five to seventy-five with one menu. In many cases it is best to stick to the simple and familiar; limit innovations to one interesting dish and show your originality in presentation and garnishes instead.

Remember that regional tastes differ. While red meat may be out of favor and sushi may currently be popular in New York or San Francisco, caterers in cities such as Houston and Atlanta report that many clients still prefer traditional roast beef. (Incidentally, even in cities where red meat has supposedly fallen from grace, caterers note that beef on a buffet table always goes in a hurry.)

In an unfamiliar city, you'll do well to ask the caterer about local trends and tastes—and trust his or her judgment. If you are entertaining at a convention or having many out-of-towners at your function, it is especially important to consider varied tastes. That does not mean you should rule out an event like the lovely Japanese party on page 164; just be sure to offer plenty of recognizable and simple options for those who might prefer chicken to yellowtail.

These practical considerations should be on your mind when you review your caterer's menu recommendations. Some will present a long list of options; others will tailor a menu to your specifications. I always prefer the latter, as it is more likely to be a menu that has been thought out in consideration of the type of guests I am inviting and my budget. It is reasonable to expect the caterer to offer three menus to choose from.

Another very important point to bear in mind when composing your menu is the type of party you have planned. While cocktail parties and formal dinners are two common solutions that spring readily to mind, there are a number of different types of parties that can be planned around food, each of which requires special menu considerations. Here are some of the most popular.

THE COCKTAIL PARTY

NORMALLY, THIS IS A STAND-UP party that lasts from one and a half to two hours, starting after work, usually at a time between 5:00 and 6:00 P.M. People are expected to come in daytime business dress and the food is limited to hors d'oeuvres. Guests know not to expect a full dinner.

Hors d'oeuvre menus may begin as low as $12 per guest, but by the time you figure in the service, liquor, mixes, tax, and tips, you can expect to spend anywhere from $18 to $75 per person for a cocktail party.

As a general rule of thumb, choose six or seven kinds of hors d'oeuvres for a cocktail party, a mix of hot and cold, and allow two to three of each per person. If the budget allows, eight selections assures a bountiful choice. Caterers observe that the people likely to eat most at a party are those coming directly from work to a large party where they don't know many of their fellow guests. Those who eat least, they say, are guests at smaller parties who do know each other, since conversation takes precedence over food. Bear this in mind when planning your cocktail menus.

To create the menu, I begin by picking one meat, one fish, one cheese, and one vegetable hors d'oeuvre. Then I fill in with as many additions as the budget allows, aiming for pleasing, unusual combinations.

I also like to vary how things are served, with some of the hors d'oeuvres passed and other selections placed on a serving table as a center to draw people together. Another reason I like bountiful buffet displays is that they give a feeling of plenty. A simple cheese board laden with several kinds of interesting cheeses and a variety of breads, crackers, and fruits makes an attractive and relatively inexpensive spread.

Food for a stand-up party should be easy to eat—no bones, no mess. Think about the logistics of balancing a drink, napkin, and hors

d'oeuvres when you plan your menu. Food should be sturdy and bite-sized and should leave nothing to dispose of except perhaps a toothpick. Nothing feels more awkward than trying to stand up and eat a dish like shrimp tempura, which must be dipped in sauce,

A caterer like Joanne Segura with strong artistic skills can take simple ingredients such as fruit, cheese, crackers, and bread, *below,* **and create an opulent buffet,** *above,* **in a matter of minutes.**

eaten in several bites, and which leaves you with the tail end of the shell in your hand. And have you ever stood around desperately trying to get rid of the bones of a chicken wing at a cocktail party? Not only is this awkward, but if you do find an empty plate, the remains are unattractive.

If you want to be sure your cocktail party foods are practical, do a trial run with a napkin and a filled wineglass in your hand. Eliminate foods that don't pass the stand-up test.

Another important thing to remember at any stand-up party is that people need to be able to put down their food, napkins, or an empty glass without returning to clutter the bar or buffet table. The best option is to have enough waiters to clear such things away on a tray; if this is not possible, provide plenty of small side tables for this purpose.

If your caterer presents you with a long list of choices rather than specific recommendations, narrow the selection by asking him which items he considers his particular specialties.

THE COCKTAIL BUFFET

THE WORDS "COCKTAIL BUFFET" ON an invitation imply a more festive party and a more generous menu, one that may serve as dinner. Usually held from 6:00 to 9:00 P.M., this kind of event can offer fewer hors d'oeuvres than a cocktail party, since you will also have a buffet table with hot foods. Because this kind of party goes on longer and runs later, dress may vary. Some guests will come directly from work; others may go home and change to party clothes.

Since more substantial food is served at a cocktail buffet, it is advisable to have some tables and chairs placed where people can sit for a while, even though the menu should be mostly finger foods that can be handled easily standing up and are easy to cut with a fork. Again, a test run with a filled glass in one hand and a plate and napkin in the other is helpful.

Cocktail buffets are popular because they are informal and because guests can choose how long they want to stay. Another advantage is the wide price range, anywhere from $20 to $100 per person, depending on how much food is served.

Miniatures of favorite foods such as quiche, pizza, shish kebab, or skewered chicken teriyaki are popular cocktail buffet fare, and many buffets feature a carver slicing roast beef or turkey for miniature sandwiches on small soft rolls. This kind of minimeal suits the present trend for "grazing." Spanish tapas, a sampling of many Spanish delicacies, is another twist on this idea. And miniature desserts are enticing; consider tiny key lime pies or bite-sized strawberry or blueberry tartlets.

A chef serving up pasta that can be topped with a choice of sauces is a relatively economical hot buffet option that lots of people enjoy. I've also seen an Oriental chef twirling Chinese noodles at a buffet, to the delight of guests.

The most lavish cocktail buffets feature a number of food stations, each offering a different type of enticing fare. This allows for smoother traffic flow and creates an atmosphere of fun. Remember you want to do whatever you can to get

guests mixing and mingling.

There are many ways a chef can create drama and fun by cooking or creating foods while guests watch. The more flourish, the better! Here are some suggestions:

- crêpes or omelettes with a variety of fillings
- potato bar offering baked potatoes with a choice of toppings from chili to crème fraîche and caviar
- croissants with a choice of sandwich fillings
- chili bar with an array of condiments—cheese, onions, sour cream, etc.
- Oriental stir-fry wok station—an especially good idea when you want to offer vegetarian options on your menu
- sushi and sashimi fashioned by a Japanese chef
- New Orleans po' boys—French

Sometimes something as simple and showy as jumbo shrimp or freshly shucked oysters is more appreciated by guests than unfamiliar exotic delicacies.

bread baguettes stuffed with fresh fried oysters, lettuce, tomatoes, and mayonnaise
- Philadelphia cheese steaks—hero rolls stuffed with steak, fried onions, and melted cheese
- New York hero sandwiches— hero rolls stuffed with cold cuts, provolone cheese, and shredded lettuce
- Chesapeake crab cakes grilled to a golden brown on a skillet and served on a soft bun
- empanadas—Mexican turnovers stuffed with meat, etc.
- Texas barbecue sliced and served on a bun with cole slaw
- old-fashioned potato pancakes, pan-fried to order and served with applesauce, mushrooms, and sour cream
- Mexican tacos with fillings to order
- Russian blinis or blintzes with a choice of sweet and savory fillings—caviar is especially nice
- Greek gyro sandwiches made with spiced lamb and salad
- Japanese steak, sliced and prepared on the grill by a hibachi chef
- grill stations for a variety of dishes that may be served on rolls or eaten with the fingers, such as thin breasts of chicken, steak teriyaki, Italian sausage, or skewers of seafood and vegetables.

When you are planning a buffet menu, whether hors d'oeuvres or dinner, keep in mind that people head first for the most extravagant foods, such as caviar or smoked salmon. If you want to serve that kind of delicacy, be prepared to serve a *lot* of it.

Don't, however, feel obliged to fill out your buffet table with big bowls of cold chicken, tuna, or pasta salad. Caterers report that people ignore these in favor of more interesting fare. If you want to serve salad, one pasta and one green salad are usually enough.

Neither cold nor hot foods should be allowed to sit out on a buffet too long. If the party spans several hours, it is better to set out small portions and replenish frequently. Many caterers warn against using chafing dishes to keep food warm because the food continues to cook all evening.

THE BUFFET LUNCHEON OR SUPPER

I OFTEN PREFER TO SERVE A LUNCH OR dinner buffet style, even if guests will eat their meal seated at tables. A buffet allows guests to mingle

Sushi makes an attractive and colorful presentation, but make sure to include some options with cooked shrimp, salmon, or vegetables for those who are squeamish about raw fish, *opposite.* Careful placement of food stations is a way to maintain a lively traffic flow and encourage guests to mingle, *below.*

more freely than at a waiter-served dinner and eliminates the need for assigned seating, which sometimes causes ruffled feelings. You should, however, still be sure to assign a staff member to each table.

There are other advantages to serving buffet style. You often can get away with a simpler menu, eliminating the first course. You will need less service help for a very large crowd than at a seated dinner. However, be careful. Many hosts who choose a buffet over a seated meal, assuming it will be cheaper, learn that this is not necessarily the case. At a buffet, portions are unlimited, selection is greater, and there is more waste; hence, a set meal may actually prove *less* expensive than a very lavish buffet. Before you make a decision based on economy, discuss the options with your caterer and get comparative prices.

Your invitation should make clear that a buffet meal will be served. A buffet luncheon can run from 12:00 noon to 2:30 P.M., allowing guests to come at their convenience. A buffet dinner starts later than a cocktail buffet, usually between 7:00 and 8:00 P.M. Unlike a less formal cocktail buffet, this invitation should give a starting time only, since guests are expected to stay for the meal. While cocktails and hors d'oeuvres should precede the meal, you will need fewer choices—three or four rather than six or seven.

The buffet menu should be more substantial than that of a cocktail buffet. Usually, there are three main-course choices—fish, meat, and chicken—plus salads and hot side dishes. Foods that make a handsome display make the best

buffet selections. Whole poached fresh salmon is a perennial favorite, as are platters heaped with whole small capons or Cornish hens, or large cuts of meats such as leg of lamb, veal, or roast sirloin of beef sliced to order.

If cost is a consideration, serve casserole and pasta dishes. This does not have to mean a dull or stingy menu. Many casseroles can be both elegant and economical.

A lavish display of fresh fruit on the buffet table is striking and can serve as a first course, as a side dish, or as dessert for those who are watching their weight. It also helps to create the bountiful look I strive for.

Desserts are usually set up separately, along with coffee, when guests have almost finished the main course.

If you *are* thinking of serving buffet style, consider the number of buffet tables you need to set up. There is nothing more annoying than standing in a long line waiting to get food. If you have more than one hundred people, you will definitely need a second buffet area. The same rule holds true for bars.

THE FORMAL LUNCH OR DINNER

THE MOST FORMAL PARTIES ARE SIT-down affairs at which several courses are served. Whether to serve lunch or dinner depends on your purpose. Luncheons may appeal to people who don't necessarily want to attend business functions in the evening. Many companies today also like to use a luncheon invitation to bring clients and prospective clients into their offices, hiring a caterer to prepare and serve an elegant lunch right on the premises.

At times only a formal setting, with all the appropriate silver and stemware, *opposite,* will do.

If you choose to give a luncheon, remember that the business day is limited and keep it short—no more than two hours. Nicholas Baxter, who caters many business luncheons in New York City, says he aims for menus that allow the guest to be in and out of the dining room in fifty-five minutes, so that guests who must leave early can do so.

Luncheons generally consist of three courses: appetizer, entree, and dessert, sometimes with a salad added. The menu should be both satisfying and light; few people like to go back to the office feeling stuffed. In cold weather, an interesting soup makes an excellent first course. In summer, cold dishes are appropriate. Here again, poached salmon is a popular main course, as are veal dishes and chicken. Formal dinners may be far more elaborate, of course, with appetizer, soup, fish and meat courses, salad, cheese, and dessert.

The type of service you choose also determines cost. Rates will go up if you decide on French service, which means serving each individual at the table from a silver tray, as opposed to plate service, where the plates are assembled in the kitchen before they are delivered to each guest at the table.

Both luncheon and dinner menus can vary considerably, according to individual budgets and tastes and the cooking style of the caterer.

Creative caterers today can cook for all tastes and are constantly changing and expanding their menus. Part of the art of choosing a pleasing meal is in combining foods that complement each other. If your caterer presents you with three prospective menus, feel free to mix and match elements from

Seating Charts and Lists Make Table Assignments Easier

Allow plenty of time to plan for seating at a large dinner; it's a complex job. Take into consideration who will be the company host of the table. And intersperse staff members evenly among the guests. If there are several guests of honor at your event, rotate them to a different table between the main course and dessert. You may also want to switch one staff person from each table. Here are the steps for planning seating arrangements:

- *On a large sheet of paper, draw enough large circles or rectangles to represent all the tables as they will be placed in the room.*
- *Make two alphabetical guest lists. Your master list should combine men's and women's names, while the second list should note male and female guests separately, with plenty of room between each name.*
- *Cut out the names from the second list into small paper tabs and attach to table plans with Scotch tape, switching around until you have a satisfactory arrangement.*
- *Give each table a number and transfer the numbers to your master guest list, which will be kept at the door.*
- *From the table plans, make out place cards, keeping them grouped by table, to be set at each place on the day of the party.*
- *From the master list, make out cards with names and table numbers to be given to guests as they arrive. Keep the cards in alphabetical order to make it easier for guests to locate their table assignment.*

each of them if you like.

An important point: always have a special fish or vegetarian dinner available for those who do not eat meat or who observe special diets. (These guests should have alerted you ahead of time.) However, save these special meals to be served last, in case other people at the table ask for the same!

A final word about dinner menus: more is not necessarily better, and a formal meal is not always the only choice. Victoria Campbell Kirsten, who caters many VIP dinners at the Whitney Museum in

With very large gatherings, assembling plates in the kitchen makes the service more efficient, especially when the entree must be piping hot, *opposite*.

Seating at a Formal Dinner

Guests at formal business functions are seated in accordance with their importance.

At a formal dinner with a head table, the host and spouse or co-host are seated at opposite ends of the table. When there is no head table, they are seated at separate tables.

When spouses or guests are invited, seating should alternate males and females wherever possible. Couples are never seated next to each other. If spouses are not present, guests are seated strictly according to importance, not according to gender.

Sample Seating Charts for Events When Couples Are Invited

Host

Most important female	2nd most important female
3rd most important male	4th most important male
4th most important female	3rd most important female
2nd most important male	Most important male

Hostess

Sample Seating Chart for Events Without Spouses

Host

Most important guest	2nd most important guest
5th most important guest	6th most important guest
4th most important guest	3rd most important guest

Co-host

New York, reports she got raves at a dinner for then–Vice President George Bush by serving a simple shepherd's pie. Her chicken pot pie supper was an equal hit with England's Princess Margaret. Those who are fixtures on the banquet circuit often love a change to warm, homey, simpler fare, Kirsten advises. And, she adds, "people who are out constantly love parties that are finished by 10:00 P.M. Top bananas relish a quiet evening."

AN EVENING OR LUNCHTIME EVENT IS not the only way to entertain. You can often save money and please people at the same time by choosing less conventional party menus. A lavish breakfast is a great way to start the day. Busy executives particularly appreciate a buffet breakfast scheduled early at a fine restaurant or hotel. Teas such as the one pictured on pages 24–25 provide a gracious and welcome break near the end of the day. On a summer day, picnics can be a treat—even indoors in a creative setting. Midnight suppers are enticing, and nothing is more elegant than a splendid dessert and champagne party. Following is a potpourri of ideas for creative entertaining.

● **A VICTORIAN MIDNIGHT SUPPER.** New York Parties served an elegant New Year's Eve supper menu to 2,800 people who attended a benefit for Carnegie Hall billed as *An Evening of Victorian Songs and Music,* part of the celebration of the hall's restoration. Following the concert, the stage was transformed into a Victorian parlor, with tea tables swathed in red velvet and creamy lace, adorned with Victorian-style decorations. The period menu featured assorted tea sandwiches with baby shrimp, salmon, and herb chicken; miniature savory tarts and a Victorian dessert extravaganza.

● **AN INDOOR PICNIC.** What to do when dinner must be fitted in before a night at the theater? Caterer Melanie Ress solves the problem neatly by serving this quick but elegant cold menu. Stylish picnic bags are set at each place, allowing guests to listen to an informative talk about

the play they will be seeing without the interruption of dinner waiters. Dessert cookies and assorted sweets are passed at each table.

● **BRUNCH IN THE COUNTRY.** A menu Ridgewell's of Philadelphia has offered includes a continental mixed grill of thickly sliced bacon, tender chicken livers, and baby lamb chops; peach halves broiled with chutney; fresh corn fritters served with sweet butter and maple syrup; quail eggs wrapped in peppery sausage; icy melon wedges; wicker baskets spilling apple walnut and orange date muffins; ginger marmalade; apricot cream cheese strudel; pecan caramel rolls; and freshly brewed coffee.

● **A BREAKFAST MENU.** Ridgewell's also

likes to offer a quartet of breakfast choices, all ending with coffee with cream and sugar: a homey country kitchen spread, elegant Continental fare, a hearty, bracing "rise and shine" menu, and a Seventh Avenue special of bagels with cream cheese.

STOCKING THE BAR

THERE ARE TWO OPTIONS WHEN IT comes to buying liquor for a party. If you purchase it yourself, you will pay less but you will also have the responsibility for selection, seeing that it is delivered on time, and arranging credit for unopened bottles. If you want the caterer to take care of this for you, expect to pay a surcharge for the service. Many caterers are happy to allow

For breakfast, Lavin Caterers worked with a florist to devise these striking buffet baskets chock full of muffins, croissants, and fruit. Fresh squeezed pink grapefruit juice and steaming cups of coffee completed the light but lovely menu.

you to save by buying the liquor yourself, but you should still let the caterer handle the bar setups and arrange for bartenders. Often the bartender will double as a waiter or helper during dinner.

Be sure you have enough bartenders to take care of guests without traffic jams at the bar. One bartender for every fifty guests is reasonable. Never serve a lot of liquor without food. At a dinner party, guests should be seated for the meal no more than an hour after the party has begun, to keep liquor consumption under control.

As a rule, people consume two to three drinks during the first two hours of a party, less after that. A liter bottle of hard liquor (33.8

ounces) contains about twenty-two 1½-ounce drinks; a liter of wine fills about ten 3-ounce glasses. Be sure the bartender pours all liquor with a 1½-ounce jigger so that drink amounts will be uniform.

● **REGIONAL DIFFERENCES.** Drinking tastes and fads may vary from one area to another. If tequila is popular in your area, you may want to add it to your liquor supply. I was reminded of the difference in regional tastes at a party in Houston. In Texas, we were told, Scotch is still the favorite drink. "Perrier is coming in," said caterer Sharon Graham, "but we're not sure we trust it yet." In Texas, the bar remained open during dinner; in New York, wine is usually con-

At the Italian Trade Commission show, guests were invited to sample Italy's fine wines along with some traditional foods.

sidered appropriate with dinner, and those who want something stronger must order it from a waiter. Check on local customs if you are entertaining in a new city.

Instruct the bartenders as to when the bar is to be closed, for both cocktail parties and seated events. Otherwise, you may find your costs over budget. Reopening the bar after dinner is optional. At formal affairs, an after-dinner cordial may be offered.

In a restaurant or hotel, be sure to alert management to your wishes. At a hotel, you should pay only for the bottles actually used; unopened bottles are returned, as at a liquor store. While you may supply your own liquor at a hotel or restaurant, you may encounter a stiff charge for the hotel's glasses, ice, and mixers.

● **DINNER WINES.** Your caterer or liquor store owner should be able to suggest appropriate wines to complement your menus. Both a red and a white should be available at dinner, whether it is a buffet or a sit-down affair. If different wines are served with each course, the lighter and drier come first. Be sure the caterer has instructed and rehearsed waiters in the proper way to serve wine. At a seated dinner, a small amount of wine is poured into the glass of the host, who sips it and nods approval to the waiter. The wine is then poured into each glass—never more than half full.

Your caterer or a knowledgeable liquor store owner should be able to suggest appropriate wines and glassware for the occasion. Many large stores have party planners on staff who can help you decide how much you need for your gathering.

	BOTTLE SIZE	SERVING SIZE	NUMBER OF SERVINGS IN BOTTLE	AVERAGE SERVINGS PER PERSON
Table wine	750 ml.	3 oz.	8	2
Champagne	750 ml.	3¼ oz.	7	2
Dessert wine	750 ml.	2½ oz.	10	2

What's Behind the Well-Stocked Bar

● **ESSENTIALS**
- *Vodka*
- *Gin*
- *Scotch*
- *Brandy*
- *Light and dark rum*
- *Sweet and dry sherry*
- *Blended whiskey*
- *Canadian whiskey*
- *Bourbon*
- *Sweet and dry ver-mouth*
- *Red and white wines*
- *Regular and light beer*
- *Campari*
- *Aperitifs: Dubonnet, red Cinzano, Lillet*

● **EXTRAS**
- *Cream sherry*
- *Liqueurs*
- *Cognac*
- *Champagne*
- *Triple Sec*
- *Tequila*
- *Port*
- *Irish whiskey*
- *Amaretto*
- *Irish Cream, other cream liqueurs*
- *Crème de Cassis*
- *Kümmel*

● **EQUIPMENT AND SUPPLIES.** *If you are setting up a bar in a location that is not usually used for entertaining, double-check to see that it is fully equipped. The bartender(s) will need the following:*
- *Jigger*
- *Corkscrew*
- *Cocktail shaker*
- *Pitcher of water*
- *Pitcher with long-handled stirring spoon*
- *Small cutting board and knife*
- *Juicer*
- *Strainer*
- *Blender*
- *Measuring spoons*

● **GARNISHES**
- *Whole lemons, limes, and oranges*
- *Precut lemon and lime wedges*
- *Curls of orange and lemon peel*
- *Cocktail cherries*
- *Olives*
- *Pearl onions*
- *Orange bitters*
- *Aromatic bitters*
- *Grenadine*

Mixers should include tomato and fruit juices, ginger ale, club soda, mineral water, bitter lemon, tonic water, and soft drinks. Have plenty of these last on hand, for they will be ordered on their own as well. There are more and more nondrinkers these days, especially on the East and West coasts.

Light punches are also popular and economical additions to a bar selection.

A well-stocked bar takes into account many tastes, including those who prefer soft drinks or mineral water as well as mixed drinks, *above.* Premixed Bellinis, *right,* are easy for summer parties.

PRESENTATION COUNTS

WHETHER YOUR PARTY IS FORMAL OR informal, presentation is every bit as important as the food itself. Don't just decide on a menu—discuss in detail how it will be set up and served. Attractive serving dishes, distinctively garnished trays or plates, a sense of plenty, and frequent, friendly but unobtrusive service all make people feel cared for and pampered. It is a feeling that is the hallmark of a successful party.

The most memorable parties are planned with a sense of showmanship that begins in the kitchen and is carried through by the serving staff. Discuss the dress, grooming, and training of the staff with your caterer. Party waiters are usually free-lancers, but I've noticed that a good caterer works with the same people regularly. Many caterers, especially on the East and West coasts, like to use actors who are between parts because they make attractive and poised servers. There are agencies that specialize in this kind of party help.

Be sure your waiters have been well trained. They should be familiar with the menu and able to answer questions about the food if asked. If you have important guests at a head table, it is a good idea to check who will be serving them. One caterer told me an almost-horror story of discovering ten minutes before a political party that the waiter assigned to the head table could barely speak English. Since the ability to communicate is absolutely essential for key service personnel, she had him transferred to a less-critical post.

Having enough waiters is crucial. Plan on one waiter for every

twenty-five people when hors d'oeuvres are passed, one for each fifty (in addition to the servers) if food is set out buffet style. This doesn't account for help in the kitchen washing glasses and plates or picking up used glassware while the party is in progress.

For dinner parties, one waiter per table, plus one busboy clearing and replenishing wineglasses, is ideal. Many hosts settle for one busboy for two tables and sometimes one waiter for two. If you have more than fifty guests, you may want to add a maître d' or supervisor to keep things running smoothly.

A touch of the dramatic in the service helps set an elegant tone for a dinner party. Having a dozen or more waiters make an entrance at once bearing trays, for example, makes more of an impression than having them come out one at a time.

An attractive, well-trained serving staff adds style and sophistication to an event.

Flying High in California

THE PROMISE OF nonstop dancing and an all-out dessert menu that featured four separate and lavish food stations were the highlights of the big party held at the annual American Booksellers Association (ABA) convention to launch Judith Krantz's blockbuster new novel. Even the inauspicious address—an empty airplane hangar —didn't deter more than 1,500 guests from kicking up their heels into the wee hours.

WHO

THE CROWN
PUBLISHING GROUP
AND BANTAM BOOKS

WHAT

DANCING AND
DESSERT PARTY

WHERE

JOHN WAYNE AIRPORT,
COSTA MESA, CALIF.

WHY

PUBLICATION
OF THE NOVEL
TILL WE MEET AGAIN

Convention entertaining brings special considerations. Often companies are competing to attract the same clients and customers, and a dancing party can be an ace card; after spending all day inside with no outlet for exercise, people welcome the release and fun of active participation.

However, just because music is the main event, food should not become secondary; this sumptuous dessert spread was an impressive but relatively inexpensive way to host a large crowd (as is often the case at industry trade shows) without weighing them down.

I've learned that after a day in a convention hall surrounded by lights, noise, and a barrage of products, people gravitate to fresh air. In the past, when the weather allows, I've gone out of my way to find spaces with gardens or courtyards. In this case, the open area was a bit different—it was in front

Working in a bare space, like the airplane hangar, *right,* often means you must bring in everything from electrical wiring, sound systems, and lighting to wall or even floor coverings.

Grapevines, trellises, barrels and casks, garden flowers, and full-sized trees, *above,* helped to re-create the look of the champagne country featured in Judith Krantz's book.

of a transformed airport hangar!

The location came from party planner Pat Ryan. After seeing her work at the Minolta party shown on page 68, I put Pat's name at the top of the list in my party file. When the ABA was scheduled for Anaheim, California, I knew immediately whom to call.

A new novel from the author of four straight best-sellers is automatically welcomed by booksellers, but they sometimes take its success for granted. The purpose of this party was to excite them about

Red velvet, a gold proscenium, and intimate seating re-created a Parisian cabaret, *left.* Buffet tables were draped with brocades, velvets, and lamé swags and adorned with silken tassels and gilt cherubs. Pedestals, ornate silver, and floral serving garnishes emphasized the elegance. *Below left,* street signs set the tone for a swanky Hollywood nightclub scene, while peasant breads, fruit, and wildflowers gave a French country look, *below right.*

Judith Krantz's latest book, to entice them to read it and become enthusiastic about promoting it.

Working with my staff, Pat came up with an intriguing plan. A hangar was a natural setting for the aviation theme and provided plenty of dancing space for the crowd of 1,500 expected. Inside, the cover and pages of the book literally came alive. Each corner of the room featured a vignette from the novel. The mood shifted from Paris to the French countryside, wartime England to Los Angeles in

The vintage World War II Spitfire airplane, *above,* served a dual purpose—making a dramatic statement to arriving guests, as well as providing a focal point for an outdoor seating group added at the last minute to accommodate overflow guests. The lure of a spectacular party *and* a famous author drew national media coverage, *right.*

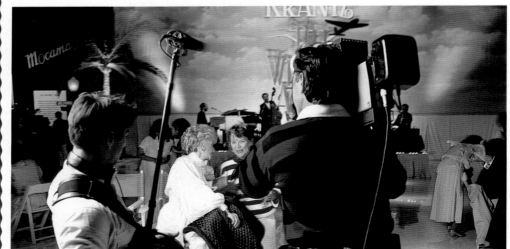

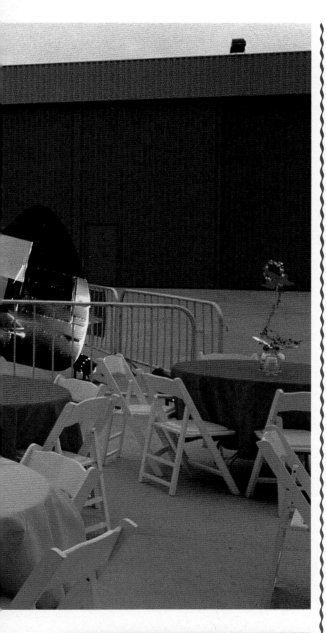

the 1930s and '40s. Decor, props, costumes, and food fit each theme; passages relating to the scene were the backdrop.

A wall painted with an 18-by-50-foot cloud scene taken from the book's jacket was behind center stage, with the jacket typography and a pink foil replica of the plane from the cover suspended in front. Matching pink and blue lights bathed the band and singers on-stage. The music was continuous, progressing as the night went on from 1940s and '50s tunes to rock, and the dance floor became more crowded with each set. At the end of the evening, many people lingered, sorry to see the party end—the surest sign of success.

I learn from every party I give, even those that are smash hits with guests. In this case it was the transportation information in the invitation that could have been improved. It wasn't clear that buses would be returning to the convention site throughout the evening; some people feared being "stuck." Also, local people sometimes assume too much when they give driving directions to newcomers. We did not do a test run of the directions until we arrived for the convention—too late to learn they were not explicit enough. Next time I will include a map.

But small miscalculations don't mar a party that succeeds in its important goals. Dozens of book-sellers came up to tell me how much they enjoyed the dancing. More important, they added that they couldn't wait to read *Till We Meet Again*. The party had done its job.

Eight full bars accommodated a large crowd without long lines for service, *left.* Careful thought goes into filling empty areas with eye-catching decor, transforming a blank canvas into a backdrop in keeping with the theme of the party, *left.*

French ballads and a cancan revue, *below,* got the evening off to a rousing start. Then the Step Sisters (Andrews Sisters look-alikes) brought back the days of the '40s and '50s, *above;* the contagious beat quickly brought everyone out on the dance floor.

Gels were used on the lights to give a pink-and-blue glow to the dance floor, *right.* The lights could be brightened and dimmed to create an interesting play on the polished white surface, and to add to the sultry mood as the night wore on. Don't be afraid to break the rules; food needn't be served by formally attired waiters. Guests loved the idea of this old-fashioned popcorn machine, *left.*

Dramatically lit palm trees and a neon Mocambo sign brought Hollywood of the '20s back to life, *right.*

"*Till We Meet Again*"
Dance Party
FOOD STATION MENU
BY ROCOCO
CATERERS

PARIS FOOD STATION
Lavish Dessert Spread:
Cakes, Pastries, Mousses

COUNTRY
FRENCH STATION
French Cheeses, Breads, Fruit,
and Pâtés

WARTIME ENGLAND
STATION
Pastry Sticks, Doughnut Holes,
Biscuits, Shortbreads, Coffee

LOS ANGELES STATION
Crêpes Suzette, Cherries Jubilee

Many of the dessert treats, *opposite,* were bite-sized so guests didn't have to be encumbered by plates and silver on the dance floor.

Serving staff at each station was costumed to match the period, like the French peasant girls, *above. Right,* a coffee-shop counter, glass jars and tin containers, ration cards, and coffee served from a spigot brought back the spirit of wartime England. At long tables with folding chairs, guests found sugar pourers, chrome salt and pepper shakers, and napkin dispensers.

The Not-So-Small Details

THE DIFFERENCE between a good and a great party is often a matter of details, seemingly small touches that add up to big impressions. Many ingredients contribute to this overall impression—lighting, music, flowers, linens and china, entertainment, and that indispensable element of surprise that sets a party apart. If one of these elements strikes a discordant note, it can undermine all your hard work.

Chapter

8

The best way I know to approach the many elements that contribute to party ambience is to do it as though I were inviting my very best friends and wanted to please and delight them in every possible way. Let's move step by step through some of the extras that help make a party stand out.

FLOWERS

THE "RIGHT" FLOWERS FOR EACH party will be different, the shapes and colors determined by the party space as well as its theme. Flowers can be romantic or sophisticated, zany or witty, elegant or country fresh. Thinking out in advance the mood you want will help the florist create in the right spirit, adding a beautiful burst of color and fragrance to the scene.

Virginia Wolff, who created these appealing wildflower bouquets for a tent party in a city park,

says that before she begins designing flower arrangements she asks her client, "How do you want to feel?" The answer for this party was "summery, refreshed," so she chose wildflowers. Because the ceiling was high, the centerpieces were made tall, imaginatively set on slim woody stems that created the look of a country garden. Hanging baskets on the tent poles carried out the feeling. Since there were many tables, the colors were kept soft in order not to overwhelm. The color choices were coordinated with the floral tablecloths, which were selected from fabric and made to order for the occasion, so the flowers became part of the overall look. This florist likes to use warm colors, such as pinks, peaches, and mauves, for the same reason that lighting designers prefer these colors—she feels the reflections are most flattering.

Go for important first impressions—an outstanding bouquet near the door, a striking overall effect seen when you first enter the room. The most important arrangements are the ones guests see when they arrive, helping to build anticipation for the rest of the party. Later, guests get caught up in conversation and notice less.

Flowers and greenery can totally transform party space. Ficus trees hung with bead lights create a romantic wonderland. Trellises or gazebos twined with flowers bring the feeling of a garden indoors. I've seen acres of green grass, benches, and streetlights brought in to turn a ballroom into a city park; palm trees, tropical blooms, and beach umbrellas artfully arranged to make a hall feel like the sunny Caribbean in the dead of winter. Hedges can

be used to divide a large space into cozier areas, creating "rooms" within a room, or to give the feeling of being outdoors in a garden.

Extravagant, well-chosen flowers, in conjunction with lighting, can be show stoppers. For the fiftieth anniversary of Central Park, Renny, one of New York's most renowned florists and party designers, had giant park scenes projected on the walls of the Cypriot corridor of the Metropolitan Museum. He placed branches of yellow forsythia on islands in the corridor's reflecting pool and bathed the entire scene in golden light casting long shadows, as if at dusk. Said one report: "The room looked the way the park sometimes looks in spring—hazy with blossoms."

It's important to have the florist visit the space, especially if it's a private home, *opposite,* before designing the flowers to make sure they complement the color scheme and furnishings.

Special Scents

Scents help to make a room inviting and add a sensuous feeling and intimacy to a party space. Roses and gardenias are among the many old-fashioned flowers that offer a bonus in their sweet fragrances, a small touch that is seldom singled out by guests but that contributes to the overall ambience of the room. If you can't achieve this with your flowers, think of other touches, such as scented candles, fragrant potpourris placed around the room, or the good smells of cinnamon sticks or cloves.

As with other party professionals, write-ups of major events in local newspapers and magazines stored in your clipping file will give you leads to talented florists.

Out of town as well as at home, a well-connected party planner should know the right florists for your needs. But while you may take recommendations to help you select a florist, do not trust anyone else to make the final decisions about the floral arrangements to be used. Talk to the florist yourself about the effect you have in mind. Look at a sketch or a sample arrangement. I learned this the hard way once when I believed a florist who said, "Just leave everything to me." As promised, his heaping bouquets were eye-catching—but that was just the problem. At the dinner party, they blocked sight lines across the table. Before long, people were quietly removing these expensive bouquets so they could talk. It's up to you to guard against this. (Notice that whenever a tall centerpiece was called for in the parties illustrated in this book, the florist took pains to use crystal-clear containers or kept the base of the arrangement narrow so that people could see across the table.)

Above: Bouquets assembled at the party site have a freer, more spontaneous look than those made up in advance and transported. Edible flowers like pansies, *left,* add a pretty touch to salads or hors d'oeuvre trays.

A Bouquet of Floral Choices

FOR SCENT	FOR HEIGHT	FOR COLOR	FOR ECONOMY
Roses	Gladiolus	Tulips	Sweet William
Gardenias	Wildflowers	Gerbera	Heather
Freesia	Snapdragons	Lupin	Miniature
Narcissus	Larkspar	Irises	Carnations
Tuberose	Flowering	Ranunculuses	Queen Anne's
	branches	Anemones	Lace

LIGHTING

GOOD LIGHTING IS INVISIBLE; GUESTS are aware only of pleasing overall ambience. Yet the right lighting can hide a room's flaws and highlight the attractive portions, can make a big space cozy or divide a room into centers of activity. Even the noise level is affected by the lighting—soften the lights and you will actually hear voices in the room lower.

To achieve flattering light, you must plan in advance. Yet because lighting is often noticed only when it is wrong, it is often overlooked in the early planning stages of a party.

To assess your lighting needs, take a hard look at your room *during the hours your party will take place*. A room looks quite different in daytime than it does in artificial light. If you are faced with hard neon or other unflattering lights,

Wiring light bulbs beneath the tables illuminated pink tablecloths and gave the whole room a sexy glow.

try turning some of them off and substituting the glow of candles. Candles almost automatically soften the atmosphere. If candles are impractical or perhaps unsafe, aim for the same soft effect through diffused lighting in warm hues, perhaps by toning down the lights with colored gels.

Failing to check the space during actual party hours may also leave you open to unexpected problems. At the Houston Historical Society fund-raiser (page 8), the host learned only as the party was about to start that fire regulations forbade extinguishing overhead lights in certain parts of the building lobby where the event was being held. For those seated in these bright sections, the magical glow of the candlelit room was lost. While the fire regulations could not be changed, the table placement could have been—if the lighting had been checked more carefully in advance.

When you have to deal with a public space that is too bright, your best bet is to call in a lighting expert who may be able to soften the existing spotlights with flattering colored gels.

Lighting can also create a mood, providing a backdrop of stark black or startling red, or casting company colors on a centerpiece. The bare columns of a museum or public building can be softened with a mix of lavender and red light; black lighting and Day-Glo paint can give a phosphorescent feel that is perfect for a nostalgic Sixties party; pink lights bouncing off the ceiling of a white tent can create the aura of a fairy tale. At a Chicago party with settings that ranged from the 1920s to the 1980s, lighting played a major role in establishing the right ambience for each era—cool blues for flappers of the Twenties, neon pink and turquoise to accent the Art Deco Thirties, and strobe lights to suggest the high-tech Eighties.

Lighting was the secret of a circus party held in an airplane hangar. The huge 30,000-square-foot hangar area was given a more intimate feeling by careful placement of theatrical lights on the rafters forty feet above. The effect was colored pools of light twenty feet in diameter that spotlighted the areas of activity while making the unused spaces seem to disappear.

The same spotlight approach can create ambient lighting for special parts of a room, to keep people circulating. Consider setting up internal arches within a room to beam light from above, drawing people toward the illuminated spaces.

Where to find the wizards who can create this kind of magic? It is the job of a good party planner or full-service caterer to know local sources and be able to call on the best specialists. That's why you pay a party planner. If you have kept a diligent party file, you may have ideas of your own as well. (See the Resource List beginning on page 202 for additional references.)

If you are not using a party planner and you want advice, I would suggest the lighting people at a local theater or the drama department of a local college. Lighting a party is not so different from lighting a stage production. In both instances, the goal is to set a scene and spotlight the important action.

Once you see what a difference proper lighting can make, you'll realize why it is worth extra attention —and expense.

A Jungle Effect

A dramatic demonstration of the magic lighting can create was the Parker House party that transformed a Boston ballroom into a jungle. The budget did not allow designer Richard Carbotti to do away with the existing formal window treatments or cover the boldly patterned carpet. But on the night of the party, they simply were not noticed by the guests because Carbotti's lighting experts, Matrix Audio, had used some twenty-six spotlights and another thirty 500-watt bulbs to focus attention on the jungle settings, making the rest of the room fade away. Artful lighting placement made the animal paintings appear to be stepping out of the dimmer background.

Accenting the Visual

Visual presentations can add a focal point to a gathering and help convey a message. The Micrographic Division of Fuji Photo Film projected a ten-minute audio-video show on a giant screen to welcome guests to New York, give them a striking sight-seeing tour of the city, say thank you for their support, and delight them with a bit of nostalgia—slides taken at Fuji events during past conventions. Many of the guests had attended these parties and could spot themselves in the photographs. This helped to strengthen the bond of good feeling between the company and its representatives, who enjoyed seeing themselves on screen. Best of all, the old photos brought laughter and a dose of fun that brightened the whole party.

Another lighting element that helped personalize this party was the use of a tinted spotlight that bathed a clear ice sculpture in the company's colors.

The professional caterer knows how to display basics with style. A silver bowl makes an elegant holder for napkins, *top;* a mound of wrapped cutlery becomes a convenient but fun buffet arrangement, *middle;* and precision-set cups, *above,* made a graphic array.

THE RIGHT RENTALS

THE RIGHT RENTALS CAN MAKE A dramatic difference in the look of your party. A rainbow of linens and myriad china, crystal flatware, and serving dish patterns are available. To get some idea of the amazing range, you need only visit the warehouse of a major metropolitan rental company like Regal Rents in Culver City or Party Rentals, Ltd., or Props for Today in New York. And since even ordinary rentals for a dinner party can add up to as much as $15 to $30 per person, it often pays to spend a little more for a special effect.

The right tablecloths, dishes, and chairs can add color, elegance, and a distinctive look to a party or carry out a theme in an imaginative way. Topping ordinary wooden chair backs with colorful cloth covers or using delicate white charivari chairs can give a dinner party a more graceful look. The use of colored serving plates can transform the mood of a table; black dishes can add a dramatic note.

If you have seen your party professional's work and trust his or her taste, you may be content to rely on the decor recommended. But it still pays to be aware of the many possibilities in rentals, particularly when you are entertaining in a private home.

MUSIC AND ENTERTAINMENT

MUSIC IS THE HEARTBEAT OF A PARTY. I've always felt it is one of the crucial elements of a great event.

It can play a variety of roles. It can be a pleasant backdrop for conversation, an inducement to get up and dance, or a sound so special that guests are compelled to stop

and listen. The kind of music you choose depends on the pace and mood you want to create. At a formal reception, a string quartet or a classical guitarist might be appropriate; a big cocktail party might call for a jazz trio or a pianist playing show tunes.

Music can add authenticity to a theme. It's fun to hear the strains of island music at a Caribbean party or a Hawaiian luau, and waiters who sing opera can add a festive surprise note to an Italian feast. And the most ordinary office party can turn into a fiesta if you serve Mexican food and have a mariachi band marching through the corridors. Colorful musicians of this kind can actually double as the evening's entertainment.

Placing musicians at a party's entrance helps you set the stage as your guests arrive. Having gospel singers outside our *Weddings* party in New Orleans put our guests in a

When musicians need a lot of electronic equipment, it is vital to check early to be sure that the wiring and outlets are sufficient.

Costumed carolers, *above,* greeted guests as they entered Crown Publishers' Christmas party, creating an instant holiday mood. This kind of surprise early in a party helps set the stage for fun. Lively jazz riffs, *opposite,* are great at an evening function when you want to wake guests up and get them moving to an infectious beat.

convivial mood before they were inside the door.

Dance music ought to have a contagious beat and appeal to all ages. Even established society orchestras like Lester Lanin's and Peter Duchin's have added soft rock to their repertoires for younger dancers. If at all possible, see and hear the band in action before you sign a contract; a tape doesn't tell you how effective they are in getting a group out on the dance floor. Dancing adds so much fun to a party that I would stretch my budget or cut back elsewhere in order to afford a really top band.

If you can't afford to hire a band, a good disc jockey can be a fine substitute. Again, try to see the person in action. You want someone who knows how to get people out on the floor and how to vary the music to keep them there.

To keep up the pace of the party, it's important and worth the added cost to see that music is continuous. Hire two bands or have a solo musician or disc jockey on tap during breaks to make sure the party's momentum doesn't die when the music stops. And if at the end of the evening everyone is clearly still enjoying the band, consider having

It's important to select music appropriate to the occasion. The lively Caribbean beat of a steel band, *above,* would be overpowering in an intimate gathering while subtle cabaret music, *below right,* would be lost in a large gathering. Tapes or records allow you to change the mood mid-party, *right.*

them play for an extra hour rather than cut the evening short. It can be well worth the expense.

Finding musicians is not difficult. If you watch local society pages, you'll begin to see the same names turning up in connection with important affairs. Whenever you come across good comments about a musical group or young entertainer, add them to your clipping file for future reference.

In large cities, there are talent agencies that specialize in music and entertainers. In every city, caterers and party planners will have knowledgeable recommendations, and almost every phone directory has listings under "Musicians."

Sources I've found invaluable for locating talented and inexpensive musical performers are music schools and music departments at colleges. Young musicians' enthusiasm often adds to their appeal and

Party Music Makers

- Dance bands
- Jazz combos
- Guitarists
- Harpists
- String quartets
- Barbershop quartets
- Pianists
- Country-Western groups
- Dulcimer players
- Bagpipers
- Flutists
- Music videos
- Folk singers
- Disc jockeys
- A cappella groups
- "Fifties" girl groups
- Rock groups
- Cabaret crooners
- Caribbean steel bands
- Rappers who incorporate company names into a commemorative song

because most are eager for the exposure their rates are usually very reasonable.

If you decide on a concert performance as your evening's entertainment, however, be careful with the timing. The proper time for the music is while the guests are still seated or assembled in a group. At the Caramoor dinner on page 28, guests wanted to dance after dinner. A predinner concert, or perhaps a pause between the first course and the entree, would have been much better received. At the Christmas party on page 158, while the guests loved the carolers at the start of the party, they were less receptive when they did a repeat sing later on during the afternoon. Again, everyone was ready to dance.

I've found one safe way to schedule entertainment and dancing at a party is to have both, but in

separate spaces. That way, guests can choose exactly what they feel like doing. But the best way I know to decide on timing is to put yourself in your guests' places.

Remember also that entertainment does not have to mean a formal act. A fortune-teller, a handwriting analyst, or a sketch artist circulating in the crowd will keep people talking and watching. Anything that makes your guests active participants in the party, whether that means doing the Charleston or having their palms read, makes them feel more involved—and makes a party better.

PARTY FAVORS

FAVORS ARE NOT ALWAYS NECESSARY at a business function. If the favors are impersonal, like paperweights or key chains with the company logo, I feel they are likely to be tossed in a drawer or the wastebasket and are not worth the expense. However, thoughtful favors can be a nice personal touch, a little bit of the party that guests can take home with them.

Such favors do not have to be expensive, but they should be unexpected and show imagination. When the favor fits the theme, like the pith helmets given to guests when they arrived at the jungle party on page 38, they can help everyone to get into the party spirit.

At fund-raisers, the typical favor is cosmetics or a small bottle of fragrance, usually donated by manufacturers or a local department store. But guests at the big Viscaya Ball in Miami, Florida, were really delighted last year to find that instead of something from the cosmetics counter, their favor

Thoughtful favors can be potent reminders of a company or product. *House Beautiful*'s stylish umbrellas, *above,* are appreciated long after the party. At the Parker House's safari party, *below,* staff members in safari outfits handed each guest a pith helmet.

bags contained wonderful breakfast treats donated by a department-store gourmet shop.

I found my guests equally pleased with homemade muffins as a favor from a party celebrating the publication of *Mary Emmerling's American Country Cooking.* Nothing could have represented the book's homey philosophy better—or brought so much goodwill the following day. At a benefit honoring director Sidney Lumet, movie film stock cans filled with cashews echoed the evening's theme. And little boxes of fine chocolates are always enthusiastically received.

Edible favors have a special warmth. So do living things like small plants or pots of herbs. And everyone appreciates creative favors that serve a really useful purpose. Guests at the Black Tie Block Party in Houston took home miniature flashlights that had been part of the table centerpieces. I'm sure they think fondly of the party every time that handy little light saves fumbling for a lock in the dark.

Visual reminders are always fun for guests. Videotape as many events as possible. It's easy, efficient, and economical, and showing the tapes at a later event is sure to bring smiles and pleasant reminiscing. You might also want to hire a professional photographer for the party and assign a staff person to show him who's who and which groupings are essential for the company archives, trade media, or simply to send to clients as mementos of the event.

Finally, if any inexpensive souvenir is guaranteed to please guests, it is a Polaroid snapshot taken on the spot and handed out in a small frame noting the date and the

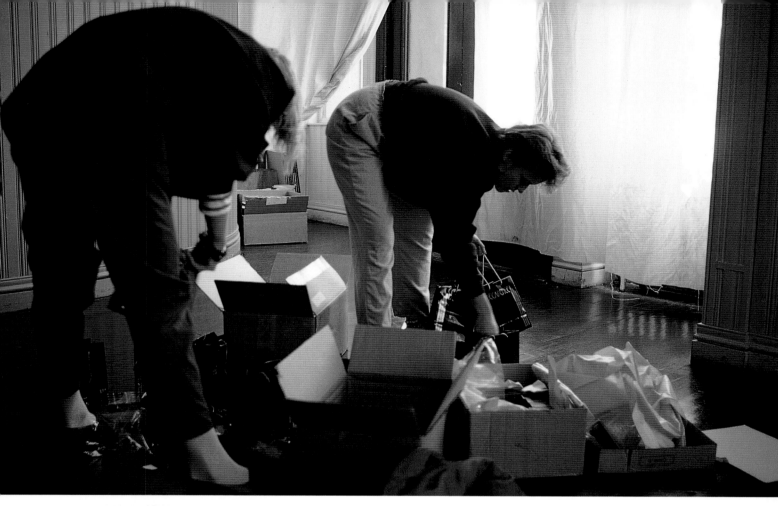

event. This is a surefire hit at employee parties. The pictures often show up on office bulletin boards, carrying the good feelings over beyond the event.

If there is a celebrity in the picture, all the better. Guests were delighted recently at a press breakfast when they were invited to be seated for a photograph at the wheel of one of the car-rental host company's jazzy 1960s convertibles, which were lined up on New York's 52nd Street. The real surprise was the passengers in the back seat—Mickey and Minnie Mouse, present as a reminder that this was the official car of Walt Disney World. The New York media turned out in force to snap pictures of the couple.

A party favor chosen with care is a final way to tell your guests you think they are special.

Often you can get favors donated if the event will generate good press or goodwill. Be creative in thinking about what would work. Each guest received a sample of Decadence perfume at the New Museum's DecaDance party, along with a souvenir yearbook, *above and left.* Polaroid photos taken during the festivities, *bottom left,* are always a hit. Cardboard frames are available directly from Polaroid.

Entertaining, Japanese Style

THE ESSENCE of Japanese design has much in common with a successful party: the combination of many small elements that create an overall impression that involves and awakens the senses. The publication of the book *Japanese Style* by Suzanne Slesin, Stafford Cliff, and Daniel Rozensztroch provided a perfect opportunity to celebrate with a party showing how this formula makes for sensational entertaining.

WHO

CLARKSON N. POTTER,
INC., PUBLISHERS

WHAT

COCKTAIL BUFFET

WHERE

JAPAN SOCIETY,
NEW YORK CITY

WHY

PUBLICATION
OF THE BOOK
JAPANESE STYLE

Sushi has become so ubiquitous on the cocktail-party circuit that menu alone would not make this party special. And it was a special challenge, as many of the guests were part of the sophisticated New York design world. We needed a location that would be new to them, as well as one that would offer the feeling of serenity that is one of the most appealing features of Japanese style.

Luckily, the decision was made simple when the Japan Society called to ask the authors to address its membership. The society's building, with its large open spaces, striking indoor waterfall, and outdoor Oriental garden, needed few additions from us to inspire the perfect mood. Best of all, it was unknown to most of the guests, who found themselves entering an oasis in the heart of New York City.

The Japan Society, *top,* was both appropriate and a place that was new to most guests. The authors, *above.* Japanese chefs performing the art of sushi-making, *opposite,* added fun and drama to the buffet table.

Having two levels allowed guests to disperse so that the party space did not become overcrowded. A rock pool and a backdrop of shoji screens added serenity and elegance to the scene. Smiling hostesses in authentic and colorful Japanese costumes offered a delightful welcome. Finding music appropriate to the occasion is an important element in an unforgettable evening. Guests were introduced to the *koto,* a traditional Japanese instrument, *opposite.*

We arranged to hold our publication party following the lecture. In return for free use of the space, we agreed to provide a special occasion for the Japan Society membership by inviting those who attended the talk to join the party.

We had the choice of using a very large upstairs exhibit hall or a smaller gallery on the main floor. I opted for the smaller space. While overcrowding is not desirable, I find a filled room far preferable to one that is half empty. Having a crowd in the room lends a festive air of excitement to a party and bonds guests into a closer unit.

Choosing the right caterer is always important, but in this case the decision had special significance, for it was the expertise of Nippanache that made the party details perfect. They knew the right sources for traditional flower arrangements, musicians, and costumes for the waitresses. They

also created food displays that showed off the Japanese talent for combining simplicity and elegance. Guests were invited to explore an outdoor Japanese garden on the second floor, which added to the authenticity of the entire evening.

The highlight of the evening for most of the guests was the food— the opportunity to sample nine kinds of deliciously prepared sushi and sashimi. Colorfully attired chefs turned the food preparation into an ongoing show. The menu also included hors d'oeuvres and dishes such as beef and chicken teriyaki for those who preferred more familiar fare.

So careful was the coordination of every element—the setting, scents, sounds, tastes, and textures —that guests soon lost sight of the individual details. They only knew that for one special evening they had stepped into the serene and perfect world of Japanese style.

Japanese Style Menu

BY NIPPANACHE
CATERERS

Japanese Hors d'Oeuvres Platter

Deluxe Sushi/Sashimi Assortment

Assorted Maki Rolls

Japanese Style Beef

Chicken Teriyaki

The heart of Japanese entertaining style is in the perfect details, from artful food arrangements to color-coordinated chop-sticks, plates, and napkins, *top, above, and right.* Each platter was designed for eye as well as appetite appeal.

Parties and Publicity

Chapter 9

BOOK PUBLISHING depends on publicity more than many industries, but there is no business that is not concerned with good press relations. If you are fortunate enough to get media coverage for your parties, you will have gained invaluable public exposure for your company. Entertaining is also an effective way to cultivate the goodwill of members of the media, goodwill that often proves helpful to you long after the event itself recedes into memories.

Two kinds of parties involve publicity: those held with the hope of gaining media coverage and those given expressly for the media. Because the goals of each are so different, I'll address them separately.

PARTIES FOR PUBLICITY

THE FIRST ADVICE I WOULD GIVE anyone who is thinking of spending a lot of time and energy on a party strictly because they hope it will appear on TV or in the press is this: don't do it.

Media exposure by itself is not sufficient reason for a party. The results are too unpredictable. Parties, even great parties, are not hard news. There is no way to know how your event will strike an assignment editor or what your competition will be on the big day. You can spend months planning the event of the decade, yet if a fire or a plane crash or a national news event comes along on the night of your party, there may be no extra camera crews around to cover your event.

Public relations, not just publicity, should be your main party goal, and you should make it clear to everyone in the company. Never, *never* promise media coverage, because you won't always be able to deliver. What you *can* promise—and what you should aim for—is goodwill and good word of mouth from your guests.

With that in mind, do include influential people and opinion makers —including the press—on your guest list. But take care to invite media people because you think they will have a good time; don't ask people only because you want them to write about you. Then, coverage or not, you will have accomplished your primary public relations goal. Media coverage becomes simply icing on the cake.

● **IMPROVING THE ODDS.** Having begun with that caveat, there are concrete steps you can take to better your chances of media coverage:

- consider the timing of your event. Television crews are scarcer on weekends, and most press people don't like to attend business functions on their days off. Your odds of coverage go up if you schedule your party for the middle of the week.
- include a "media event," something unique that offers photo opportunities for newspapers or

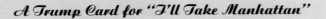

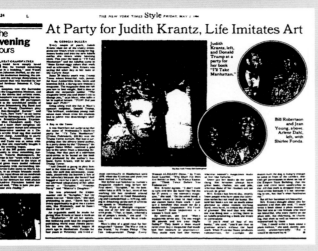

Author Judith Krantz creates dream worlds, worlds where everyone is handsome and rich and life is filled with luxury and glamour. Trump Tower, the fictional home of the heroine in Krantz's I'll Take Manhattan, *provided a party setting that could have been a scene from the novel. The glittering black-tie champagne and dessert party, with dance music provided by Peter Duchin's orchestra, brought out New York's "beautiful people" in large numbers—along with TV crews and press corps.*

There were plenty of celebrities to keep the cameras busy, but the trump card for the media was Donald Trump himself. He appeared in person to hand the key to the Tower to author Krantz.

television. Wrapping the Mint Building in New Orleans like a wedding gift, as we did to commemorate Martha Stewart's book *Weddings*, was a photo lure as well as a pleasant surprise for our guests.

Let assignment editors know about your event. Send out a release labeled Photo Opportunity, a short, enticing paragraph describing what will take place and the *exact* time it will occur. And include a contact name and number at the company for further information. Reporters and photographers don't have time to hang around a party waiting for something to happen. They need to know just when to appear—and they need to be able to find out in advance just what to expect.

Be careful not to promise something you cannot deliver; the media resents false alarms.

I always have someone on my

An assignment notice, *right*, lets media people schedule their time efficiently, and helps ensure a good turnout.

CROWN NEWS

FOR IMMEDIATE RELEASE
CONTACT: Amy Malsin
254-1600 ext. 783

ASSIGNMENT NOTICE

DATE: Wednesday, April 30, 1986
TIME: 9:00 p.m.
PLACE: The Trump Tower Atrium
725 Fifth Avenue

EVENT: JUDITH KRANTZ TAKES MANHATTAN

Some of New York's brightest lights will shine for best-selling author Judith Krantz when she takes Manhattan at the Trump Tower on Wednesday evening, April 30th at 9:00 p.m. Co-host and personal friend, Donald Trump, has helped stage [a lav]ious welcome which promises Judy her own scaled-down version of the [even]ing, bright lights to rival Broadway's, and a presentation to [Trump] Tower. With the expertise of David Lees, the prominent [atrium] by sparkling trees studded with white chasing [lights, e]ach of the stores residing in the presti[gious] f grandness that not even Maxie, [ ] the Trump Tower, could [ ] and his orchestra [ ] evening staff phone the day before the event, just to make sure the announcement has not gotten lost in the office mail. Also, a little personal enthusiasm never hurts.

● **MEDIA DRAWS.** What brings out the media? Celebrities. If your celebrities are colorful, or you can get them to do something unexpected for the cameras, like Donald Trump giving Judith Krantz the key to Trump Tower at our *I'll Take Manhattan* party (opposite), your odds for coverage also increase.

I mentioned earlier that the New York media turned out when Mickey and Minnie Mouse showed up as passengers in classic convertibles. The characters weren't news; the way they were presented was.

I've been fortunate enough to have celebrity authors who are a publicity director's dream. We didn't have to worry about attracting media for unconventional author Tama Janowitz. As the setting for the publication party for her book *A Cannibal in Manhattan,* she picked the nightclub Trader Vic's, a wild setting full of skulls and spears. The TV editors knew they could count on outrageous Tama not to disappoint them, and she didn't. She showed up wearing a strapless tulle costume—and a bone in her hair. The party got national coverage on "Entertainment Tonight" and was featured on local television news as well.

If you don't have a big-name celebrity, be creative in coming up with a focal point. Think about what makes a good visual story. An unusual fashion show or a unique product demonstration may do the trick. Corny though they may sound, cook-offs, crazy birth-day cakes, ten thousand balloons being launched, and the world's largest *anything* are events that often seem to make their way to the television screen because they offer colorful visual shots. The trick is to give a fresh slant to some of the old standbys.

Giving your event an aura of fun will often interest the media. We had good coverage for a relatively low-budget party launching a book called *Food by Phone,* a directory of New York restaurants that deliver. With cooperation from the telephone company, we found a space inside their offices. And we convinced several of the chefs whose restaurants were featured in the book to come and prepare their specialties on the spot. Guests were treated to everything from Chinese dumplings to cookies to pizza.

Enlisting chefs in action is a good bet for coverage, and looking for a local angle always helps. Our *Weddings* party in New Orleans, where well-known area chefs offered their best desserts, is another good example.

When you are aiming for media coverage, remember that there are many sections of a newspaper and many categories of magazines that might be tapped. Your menu might provide a story with a food slant. Interesting flowers might merit attention from the garden editor or a gardening publication. The business side of entertaining is a relatively unexplored avenue, and an article in the business pages or in a business journal might be seen by important business contacts who don't read the social pages.

Social columnists and feature reporters are also potential outlets for items about your plans. Read

carefully to get a sense of the kind of story that interests them.

It's worth mentioning that the time to begin building good relations with the media is long before you actually hold your event. Getting to know people personally will make them more receptive to covering your events when the time comes.

● **GIMMICKS THAT BACKFIRE.** Media coverage is a plus, but going after it too aggressively can prove to be a pitfall. If you reach too far looking for photo gimmicks, you can run into trouble—and I've had my share of disasters to prove it.

One of the most embarrassing was for a humor book called *Pigs in Love*. We scheduled a "pig-nique" at Tavern on the Green in Central Park and promised the media two things they love—children and animals. We hired actors to portray amorous pigs and rented a truck full of pigs from an upstate breeder. We invited guests to bring their kids to see the fake pigs cuddling and the real pigs gamboling outside in the park. The media showed up for this one, all right, but so did Warner LeRoy, owner

of the Tavern, who firmly declared, "No pigs." The porkers had to be shipped back to the farm. Even our live hog caller wasn't enough to soothe reporters' anger. One reporter actually made a crack on the air about publicists and their false promises.

The pig-nique was fun for those who attended despite the media gaffe, but nothing went right at the party planned for the book *How to Make Love to a Man*. I had hoped to make this one fun and just a little bit sexy. We rented a theater and put a king-size bed made up with satin sheets center stage. Guests were invited to come up to have their pictures taken on the bed. Of course, I hoped the media would photograph them having their photos taken.

But it just didn't work. For starters, a theater proved to be a bad place for a party. It was too big, the rows of seats made it tough to mingle, and people tended to just sit down next to someone they knew. Everyone felt inhibited about meeting new people.

Most of all, everybody was leery of that provocative bed. The joke

The flash of paparazzi, attracted by celebrity guests, signaled glamour and excitement outside the *Vanity Fair* party.

Making a Splash with the Media

A "photo opportunity" is a must when you want to attract media coverage for a party. Author Tama Janowitz made it easy. At Trader Vic's, a perfect setting to celebrate her book A Cannibal in Manhattan, *Tama delighted photographers with her Pebbles Flintstone hairdo.*

fell flat—and so did the party. That was one time when I got carried away hoping to provide a media gimmick, and I learned a lesson I won't forget.

Remember that your first aim is to entertain the guests, not a camera crew. If your parties are planned with the warmth, creativity, and concern that ensures a wonderful time, you won't have to worry about getting attention for them. Your guests will spread the word for you.

THE PRESS PARTY

WHEN YOU HOLD A PARTY EXPRESSLY for the media, you can forget about gimmicks. You should treat media people like any other valued business associates—and entertain them accordingly.

There are a number of ways to entertain members of the press. The best are one-to-one meetings over lunch, where members of the company's public relations staff can establish personal relationships with the media people who cover the company and its field. This doesn't mean you should expect favors or special treatment in return for lunch; it does mean that a reporter or editor will be more knowledgeable about your company and more likely to recognize and cover news stories when they occur. I always find that media people have a lot to teach me about what is happening in my field too.

Beyond getting to know key media people individually, many companies like to hold small lunches on their own premises, where the press can become familiar with the company's day-to-day operations and meet more of the staff. This makes them feel more personally connected to you and your company.

At sit-down events, company officials and guests of honor should change their seats from one table to another to be sure that all the media guests have an opportunity to speak to them personally.

Members of the media are usually invited when a party is held to celebrate a new product or an anniversary, differentiated from other guests only in that they may receive a press kit giving extra details about the event. To ensure that you recognize everyone and deliver the kits, have a separate media guest list at the door. It's also a good way to keep track of who attended, since it is easy to miss people in a crowded room. Many guests find it a nuisance to carry press kits around during a party, so the most considerate thing to do is to inform people when they sign in where they can pick up press materials on the way out.

Finally, many companies hold an annual party exclusively for the media, strictly as a gesture of good-

Getting the Picture

Media photographers accomplish more when they are accompanied by a staff member who can quickly identify company officials and important guests. Assign an escort to each photographer present—including your own staff photographer.

Having a company photographer on hand is important. Pictures may be useful for placements in the trade press as well as in general publications that do not send their own representatives. They can also be sent to important guests as goodwill gestures. And shots from every party should become part of the files, available if a story on the company should ever require pictures from the past.

An Inviting Location

There is always competition for guests at a convention. When we held a party in Washington, D.C., for book reviewers during the ABA convention, the firm of Washington, Inc., helped find a private home in the exclusive Kalorama section of the city. I knew that most people had never seen this area—and that the only way to get into one of these beautiful homes was to accept our invitation. We also had the unique opportunity of having found name authors as our guests of honor, which was a great draw itself.

Beautifully landscaped grounds enhance this stately home, *far right*, which drew an enthusiastic crowd of conventioneers, *right*.

will. In planning this kind of party, it is important to remember that reporters and editors often are deluged with invitations like yours, more than they could ever find time to attend. So the challenge is to make your party special, beginning with an invitation that will be noticed among the many received. To prevent invitations from getting lost in a pile of back mail, many companies have them hand-delivered.

The invitation should convey the idea that the party is going to be special, but you should always be honest about the intent of your event. If a business announcement will be included, say so. But don't ever promise a big story just to lure guests; they may come once, but not a second time.

You will definitely increase your acceptances by choosing a desirable location. Many companies find it worthwhile to spend extra for a party space that is "in." In New York City, for example, invitations to breakfast at "21" or cocktails at the Rainbow Room began coming in as soon as these remodeled locations reopened. A lot of people wanted to see the new interiors, so they said yes to these invitations. If you hold an annual press luncheon at a fine restaurant like the Four Seasons, as Air Canada does each year, you can feel fairly confident that people will come to look forward to the event.

While I consider unique locations a good investment for companies that can afford them, I do not always have a luxury budget, so I have to be more creative. In New York, I like to seek out unusual small restaurants, places that people have started to talk about. A brand-new restaurant is another approach that attracts, offering a

Conventioneers always welcome the chance to escape fluorescent lights and crowded aisles, so we were particularly grateful that the weather held up and cocktails could be served outdoors, *left.*

preview before the general public gets in. As I've mentioned before, you do take a chance when using an unknown establishment; watch extra carefully to see that things are done right. I would never use a new restaurant for a sit-down meal —only for cocktails, where the food is less of a focal point.

Timing is important for busy media people. Most do not like to stay late for a business dinner and can only occasionally take time out for a long lunch. An elegant breakfast is a nice way to start the day without taking up too much work time. A buffet lunch often gets a good response because guests can control how long they stay.

The day of the week matters also. Tuesday, Wednesday, and Thursday are less hectic than the beginning or the end of the week, and you are more likely to get acceptances for these days.

Always follow up written invitations to the press with a personal call. Think about all those invitations in the mail. It's easy for yours to be overlooked. And your personal warmth may be just what it takes to convince someone to attend your event.

Resist the temptation for a long sales pitch at press parties; keep the speeches to a minimum. At an annual party, a brief, warm thank-you for the year's coverage is sufficient. Remember that your goal in entertaining is goodwill, not hard sell. When you have a long announcement to make, you might do better to hold a news conference rather than a party.

The same care that makes any party a success will see you through when you entertain members of the media. If you treat media people like friends, they soon will be just that.

French Flair for Givenchy

IT WAS THE FIRST DAY of Market Week for home-furnishings buyers and journalists. Editors from top home fashion publications were beginning a full week of splendid parties, yet at the very first event of the day, one was overheard saying to another, "Obviously, this is going to be the crème de la crème." This anticipation was heightened by the promise of an introduction to Givenchy himself.

WHO

WESTPOINT
PEPPERELL

WHAT

COCKTAIL RECEPTION

WHERE

A PRIVATE
TOWN HOUSE IN
NEW YORK CITY

WHY

MEDIA INTRODUCTION
OF THE NEW
GIVENCHY ATELIER
COLLECTION

The occasion was a small press reception for major editors to launch a new line of linens by noted French designer Hubert de Givenchy. Introductions are a vital step in marketing and publicizing any new product; the right event can indelibly position a product in editors' minds.

Joe Ruggiero and Risa Calmenson of WestPoint Pepperell began with a built-in advantage because Givenchy himself had agreed to appear. But that created even more pressure to come up with a location that would reflect both the elegance of this prestigious line while providing the best showcase for the merchandise. What would stand out in editors' minds when their week of parties was over?

Luckily, caterer George Prifti, whom WestPoint has used for many occasions, knew of a private town house that could have been

transplanted from Paris, one whose owner occasionally allowed it to be used for small affairs.

Everything was wonderfully French—the furniture, the fabrics, the draperies, the chandeliers, the paintings, even the books on French history and famous French-women in the library. Enhanced by candlelight, classical music, and the scent of Old World bouquets, the setting made guests feel they had been transported to Europe.

The apartment was on two levels, with a small garden outside adorned with classical sculptures. Sometimes a duplex apartment can be tricky as a party setting; if guests stay on one level and don't mingle, the party lacks cohesiveness. In this case, as one person said to another, "Have you seen this room?" or,

Merchandise can be displayed in many arresting ways, like the beautiful bed and bath settings, *opposite*. The setting was chosen to suit Hubert de Givenchy's elegant image. Sometimes less is more when you want to show off really special hors d'oeuvres, *above*.

The opportunity to meet a celebrity, *above,* gives a party special appeal, especially when the guests know they are part of a select number invited. The invitation, *opposite below,* printed on translucent stock over a powerful photograph of Givenchy, stated that the designer himself would attend. The press kit is an all-important reminder of the party and its business purpose. The linens were showcased on the owner's own antique bed, *opposite.* That the sheets held their own in this beautiful environment was the strongest endorsement the hosts could have hoped for.

WestPoint Pepperell Party for Givenchy

MENU BY
GEORGE PRIFTI

Lobster with Black Truffles en Bouchée

Sautéed Foie Gras and Mango

Ratatouille Tartlets

Veal with Lemon Chanterelles on Brioche Toast

Beluga Caviar on Toast Points

Wild Mushrooms with Beurre Blanc on Toast

French Wines, Champagne

"Have you seen that chair?" everyone kept circulating so as not to miss anything. Even sophisticated editors were not too blasé to recognize a great environment.

Since he had worked there before, the caterer knew it was possible to prepare much of the party food on the spot, so his elegant menu was planned accordingly. After the party, the staff cleaned up immediately, leaving everything immaculate. In a private home, it is important to have a ca-

terer who is sensitive to the owner. One reason WestPoint Pepperell was able to get this space was that the owner knew and trusted Prifti.

Givenchy also was obviously delighted with the setting and walked around the apartment with as much interest as the guests. The editors were pleased with the opportunity to meet him, and the intimate space made for easy conversation. The designer's warmth added a great deal to the event.

One minor miscalculation was

setting the party for 3:00 to 6:00 P.M. and stating that Givenchy would attend from 4:00 to 5:00; no one arrived before Givenchy was due, and the party ran well past 6:00 P.M.

As a last perfect touch, departing guests were given a sample of Givenchy perfume and a "catalog"— a bound book of magnificent photographs showing the complete line of sheets in spectacular European settings—a final reminder of the wonderful space they had visited.

A Final Word on Successful Parties

THE WONDERFUL PARTIES shown in this book are all quite different, but they share something in common: they are one part inspiration, ten parts attention to detail. Setting, menu, music, flowers—these are the sizzle of the party, the visible excitement. But equally important are the logistics that make guests comfortable and make the party tick, things that go unnoticed—unless they go wrong!

Chapter 10

The lobby, the elevator, the coat check, the rest rooms, the traffic flow must all be carefully considered. Even the dance floor can present hazards without advance inspection; uneven flooring or exposed wires might cause a fall.

The best way I know to ensure a near-perfect party (and remember, no party is truly perfect) is with careful advance planning and a complete run-through of the party space at least a week before the event. Let me give you just one example from my own experience where the run-through saved a party from near disaster.

We had chosen a brand-new restaurant as the location for a party announcing *Mary Emmerling's American Country Cooking* and had taken the owner's word as to how the soon-to-open establishment would look. It was taking a chance, but the setting seemed promising

and appropriate, the cost was right, and there was a certain appeal in using a location no one had seen.

When my staff and I arrived for our run-through, we were appalled to find a bare and uninviting space. The restaurant opening had been delayed, but the party could not be. What did we do? We got in touch with the author, whose home is filled with antique country collectibles and folk art, and combed our own apartments for quilts, baskets, and other accessories that would give the restaurant space a warmer feel. We decorated the walls and used big country baskets for serving the hors d'oeuvres. An innovative floral shop rented us herbal topiaries, twig baskets of potpourri, and lovely floral wreaths for the evening at a fraction of their purchase price.

I discovered a practical problem as well. When we walked through the space, we found the coat check was in the back of the room, where guests would have to fight through a crowd to reach it. I insisted it be moved to the front.

This party, which was a success, could have been a disaster without the advance run-through. Don't depend on someone else's word; check everything for yourself.

When every element of a party, from location to menu to a convivial ambience, comes together, the inevitable outcome is a good time had by all—including the hosts!

I use the checklists starting on page 202 to plan for every party, beginning months in advance, to make sure nothing is overlooked. They are the results of many years of trial and error. Using them carefully, well in advance, may spare you a lot of unnecessary last-minute angst.

Remember, however, that the real reason for attention to all these details—and the real reason for your party—is simply to show people that you care about them. If you take only one thing away from this book, I hope it will be a determination at every party to communicate to your guests that you value them and their business.

If you approach party giving in this way—if your main concern is giving your guests pleasure—you don't have to be nervous about the outcome. If you choose professionals who share this philosophy of caring about people and wanting to delight and surprise them, you can feel confident about their performances. Should something minor go wrong in spite of all your precautions, don't worry, it won't spoil the party—not when so much else will be so right.

By all means, learn all you can about the basics of party giving. Do your homework and check every detail you can. Make every effort to ensure that people will feel welcomed and comfortable. Then relax and enjoy the party along with your guests. Hopefully you will have helped your company establish better rapport and understanding with your clients, customers, and/or coworkers—which, in the end, is really what entertaining for business is all about.

A Deca-dent Celebration

THE NEW MUSEUM is unique in the New York art world, a maverick institution dedicated to innovative work by living artists. For an organization that started on a shoestring, a tenth birthday was a triumphant landmark—and it posed a special opportunity both to thank loyal supporters and attract new ones. And because the event took place at two separate locations, extra careful planning was absolutely essential.

WHO

THE NEW MUSEUM, NEW YORK CITY

WHAT

DINNER DANCE AND AUCTION

WHERE

THE PUCK BUILDING BALLROOM

WHY

TENTH ANNIVERSARY FUND-RAISER

DecaDance was a clever three-part anniversary celebration that provided maximum effect for minimum expense, using the museum itself for two of the events.

The museum staff and the benefit committee began work almost a year in advance of this important anniversary, which was to be an art event as well as a fund-raiser. They had discarded a dozen ideas before benefit chairperson Laura Skoler came up with the DecaDance theme. The double entendre lent itself to intriguing invitations and decorations in keeping with the museum's avant-garde image, while the prefix "deca" announced that it was birthday number ten.

Artists whose work has been exhibited at the museum have traditionally donated small works for an annual benefit auction. This year they were asked to help launch the museum's second decade by contributing major pieces and more

Handpainted trays, *right and opposite,* **made an artistic setting for hors d'oeuvres. A public exhibit of works to be auctioned,** *top,* **publicized the benefit and provided an opportunity to show off the museum building, an 1850 cast-iron SoHo landmark,** *above,* **to prospective members.**

than seventy-five were received.

Ultimately, the committee decided on two auctions for the night of the party. The most important works would be offered at the dinner dance. But the young collectors traditionally encouraged by the New Museum were not forgotten: a silent auction of smaller works at the museum was scheduled for the cocktail hour preceding dinner.

Both auctions gained prominence and publicity when the artworks were displayed in a four-day public showing at the New Museum preceding the benefit. A private preview of the exhibit was planned to attract top patrons.

Because the benefit evening would be so busy with the auctions and dancing, caterer Mark Fahrer planned a menu that could be served at room temperature, for flexibility and quick service. He also set up a lavish dessert buffet to

Lighting is one of the most overlooked elements of party planning—and one of the most important. Electrical technicians met early the morning of the party to double-check wiring, *below*, and to make certain that the band and auctioneer would be well lit, *above*.

The Puck Building, *right*, once housed the humor magazine *Puck*. Inside, an Art Deco bar, *above*, served as a whimsical backdrop to the dessert buffet. Spotlights softened with pink gels, *below*, bathed each table with a flattering rosy glow.

Buses to convey guests the two blocks from preview to party, *above,* were much appreciated when the weather became inclement. Florist Robert Salone's exotic centerpieces, *opposite,* included amaryllis, palms, grass sprayed with gilt paint, and pearlized monstera leaves, all crowned with a final decadent touch—mock pearls.

encourage guests to mingle.

As soon as the guests were seated, Robert C. Woolley, a senior vice president of Sotheby's, presided over the auction. A large screen was set up to show slides of the piece being offered for those who could not see it clearly— another thoughtful touch. The careful planning paid off: many of the works attracted bids of more than $20,000.

There were few things to criticize at this party. The space was original, the decor fun, and the music inviting. The building did not provide fresh drapes as they had promised, a detail that might have been checked out earlier. And the table centerpieces might have been more dramatic had they been spotlighted from above.

But considering the limited budget, the overall effect was delightful —sensual, surprising, pleasingly different, and just a little bit decadent—exactly what the DecaDance planners had hoped for.

It was a night that launched a promising second decade for the New Museum.

DecaDance Menu
BY MARK FAHRER

*Black Pasta with White Scallops,
Sun-Dried Tomatoes, and
Black Olives*

*Sliced Boneless Breast of Chicken
Stuffed with Tarragon*

*Julienned Vegetable and
Mushroom Duxelles*

Fat Asparagus

*Saffron and Wild Rice with Scallions
and Black Mushrooms*

DESSERT BUFFET

*Chocolate Mousse Cake with
Shaved Chocolate*

Viennese Pastries

Chocolate Fudge Cake

Giant Cookies

*Dacquoise with Layers of Hazelnut
Butter Cream*

*Dipped Fruits: Hot Chocolate Sauce
with Strawberries, Pineapple,
and Oranges*

Lemon Roll with Whipped Cream

To combine glamour with a touch of decadence, the black-and-red color scheme was carried through to the tablecloths and chairs and even a surprise first course of black pasta served on black plates, *left,* and a jewel-like dessert tray, *above.*

When a display is used in front of a large crowd, secondary screens help ensure that everyone has a clear view, *opposite.* Overleaf: A round table is always most conducive to lively conversations but limit guests to ten or fewer.

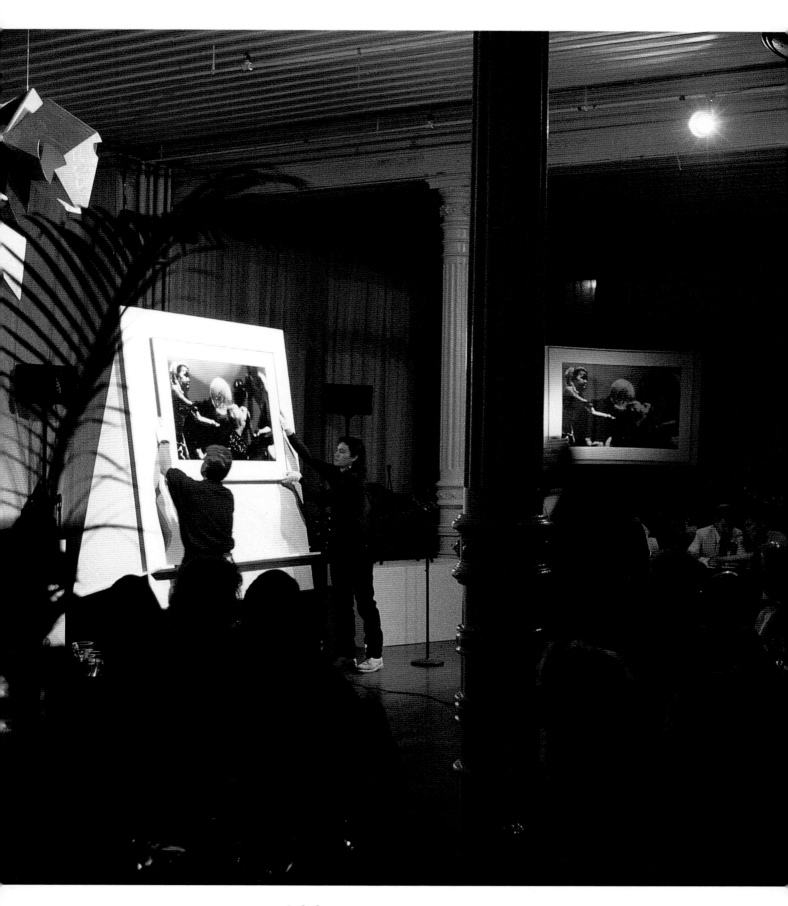

Checklists and Resources

Party Budget Worksheet

Little items can add up to big expenses. Make a separate photocopy of this budget worksheet for every party to be sure you have anticipated all potential expenses before finalizing the budget for your event. This worksheet is broken down to point out costs that are sometimes forgotten, such as postage, or cocktail napkins and matches. When you work with a caterer, many items such as service, cleanup, rentals, or ice may be included in the food fee; be sure to check on each such item so that you will not be faced with unexpected last-minute expenses.

EVENT

. . . .
. . . .
. . . .
. . . .

DATE

. . . .

TIME

. . . .

PURPOSE

. . . .
. . . .
. . . .
. . . .
. . . .

NUMBER OF GUESTS

. . . .

PROPOSED BUDGET

. . . .

PARTY SPACE

Rental fee for space . . . .
Insurance . . . .
Scenery, props, other
  decor . . . .
Flowers . . . .
Lighting . . . .
Heaters or fans . . . .
Tent . . . .

Subtotal . . . .

TRANSPORTATION (if needed)

Chartered buses or
  limousines . . . .
Refreshments for trip . . . .
Hostesses (if needed) . . . .

Subtotal . . . .

STAFF

Party planner . . . .
Party designer . . . .
Bartenders . . . .
Waiters . . . .
Cleanup help . . . .
Coat-check attendants . . . .
Parking attendants . . . .
Security personnel . . . .
Elevator operator . . . .

Subtotal . . . .

FOOD AND BEVERAGES

Caterer's menu ....
Wine/liquor ....
Mixers ....
Ice ....

Subtotal ....

EQUIPMENT RENTALS

Tables ....
Chairs ....
Dishes ....
Glassware ....
Silverware ....
Serving dishes/warmers ....
Linens ....
Vases ....
Miscellaneous ....

Subtotal ....

ENTERTAINMENT

Band or musicians ....
Entertainers ....
Disc jockey ....
Piano rental ....
Piano tuning ....
Wiring or sound system ....
Spotlights ....

Subtotal ....

INVITATIONS

Design ....
Printing ....
Addressing ....
Postage ....

Subtotal ....

INCIDENTALS

Matches ....
Ashtrays ....
Cocktail napkins ....
Bathroom towels/
  accessories ....
Name tags ....
Place cards ....
Favors ....

Subtotal ....

PUBLICITY

Press releases
  Printing ....
  Postage ....
Press kits ....
Photographer ....
Extra outside personnel ....

Subtotal ....

MISCELLANEOUS

Total sales tax ....
Service charges ....
Tips ....
Other ....

Subtotal ....

TOTALS

Combined subtotals ....
Contingency allowance
  (approximately 5%) ....

Total party expenses ....

Invitation Checklists

Use the following checklists to plan your invitation and to keep track of acceptance. The alphabetical guest list should be photocopied in multiples to provide a space for each guest. After each event these lists—together with a sample of the finished invitation—should become a permanent part of your party file. You can also use the alphabetical list to draw up the door list as well as name tags or placecards.

DESIGN

Designer's name . . . .
Name and address of firm . . . .
. . . .
Phone number (   ) . . . .
Date design submitted . . . .
Names of those approving and dates
    of approval . . . .
. . . .
. . . .
. . . .
Date finished artwork to be
    delivered . . . .
Estimate of cost . . . .
Final cost . . . .

MAILING

Person to address invitations . . . .
Address . . . .
. . . .
Phone number (   ) . . . .
Date delivered . . . .
Date due . . . .
Date returned . . . .
Person to mail invitations . . . .
Address . . . .
. . . .
Phone number (   ) . . . .
Date delivered . . . .
Date mailed . . . .
Estimates of cost . . . .
Final cost . . . .

PRINTER

Name and address of firm . . . .
. . . .
Phone number (   ) . . . .
Date job delivered to printer . . . .
Date proofs due . . . .
Date delivered . . . .
Names of those approving and dates of
    approval . . . .
. . . .
. . . .
Date finished job due . . . .
Date delivered . . . .
Estimate of cost . . . .
Final cost . . . .

TEXT

(blank lines)

Alphabetical Guest List

Party . . . .
Date . . . .
Location . . . .
Date invitation sent . . . .

CATEGORIES

• *Cus = customer;* • *D = dealer;*
• *S = staff;* • *VIP = local or national
official;* • *Cel = celebrity;* • *F = friend
of company;* • *M = print media
(newspaper and magazine);*
• *T = TV or radio.*

Name . . . .
Title . . . .
Category . . . . . Accept/Regret . . . .
Date . . . .
Address . . . .
Phone (   ) . . . .

Name . . . .
Title . . . .
Category . . . . . Accept/Regret . . . .
Date . . . .
Address . . . .
Phone (   ) . . . .

Name . . . .
Title . . . .
Category . . . . . Accept/Regret . . . .
Date . . . .
Address . . . .
Phone (   ) . . . .

Name . . . .
Title . . . .
Category . . . . . Accept/Regret . . . .
Date . . . .
Address . . . .
Phone (   ) . . . .

Name . . . .
Title . . . .
Category . . . . . Accept/Regret . . . .
Date . . . .
Address . . . .
Phone (   ) . . . .

Name . . . .
Title . . . .
Category . . . . . Accept/Regret . . . .
Date . . . .
Address . . . .
Phone (   ) . . . .

Name . . . .
Title . . . .
Category . . . . . Accept/Regret . . . .
Date . . . .
Address . . . .
Phone (   ) . . . .

Master Checklist

A master checklist that summarizes all the elements of the party is an invaluable party-planning aid. No matter how many parties you have given, using a checklist will help to make certain the next one is even better. Begin as early as possible to make major party decisions and set a date; the best people and places are booked well in advance. Use the walk-through checklist that appears on the following page to help you envision the flow of the party and spot potential trouble zones in the days (and hours) leading up to the event. Again, make a separate photocopy of this list for each party.

THREE TO SIX MONTHS AHEAD

_____ Determine the purpose of the party.
_____ Allot a budget.
_____ Set a date.
_____ Decide the number of guests.
_____ Set the theme or mood.
_____ Interview and choose a caterer and/or party planner.
_____ Select a location.
_____ Decide on music.
_____ Choose a florist.
_____ Engage a lighting specialist.
_____ Consult a party designer (for large events).
_____ Hire a photographer.

Be clear as to who is responsible for the following:

_____ Insurance
_____ Security
_____ Parking
_____ Coat check
_____ Advance publicity (for benefits or publicity events)

If a nonprofit organization is holding the function, check with the hotel or caterer about state regulations concerning sales tax. Some states waive the tax but require a certificate that must be obtained in advance.

For all the professionals that you hire, have detailed arrangements and costs in writing and signed by both parties.

TWO TO THREE MONTHS AHEAD

_____ Make out guest list.
_____ Have invitations designed.
_____ Have invitations printed.
_____ Arrange for hand-addressing of invitations.
_____ Print paper napkins/matches with company logo.
_____ Have press kits designed and printed.
_____ Select and order favors or product samples.

ONE MONTH AHEAD

_____ Mail invitations.
_____ Finalize menu.
_____ Print menu cards where appropriate.
_____ Finalize floral arrangements.
_____ Finalize decor.
_____ Write and send further news releases where appropriate.
_____ If necessary, arrange to have pianos tuned the week before the party.
_____ Check condition of dance floor.
_____ Check for any microphones, special music, or video equipment needed.
_____ Check electrical outlets to be sure they are sufficient; get adapters or extension cords where necessary.
_____ Prepare any press releases or photos to be handed out in kits.

ONE WEEK AHEAD

_____ Do follow-up phone calls if necessary to help determine accurate guest count.

_____ Make a final alphabetized guest list and media list.

_____ Prepare name tags; be sure extra blanks are on hand.

_____ Do table seat assignments and make place cards for sit-down dinners.

_____ Be sure tables have numbers or markers to identify them.

_____ Send final alert to media assignment editors.

_____ Write or telephone columnists who cover parties.

_____ Be clear with caterer about who is responsible for cleanup; assign staff members where help is needed.

_____ Arrange for funds needed to pay caterer and/or delivery vendors.

ONE DAY AHEAD

_____ Do a second run-through to be sure all needed changes have been made and everything is in place.

_____ Make final telephone calls to assignment editors.

_____ Set out table numbers and place cards on tables according to charts.

_____ Post staff members to personally escort guests inside.

_____ If needed, place directional signs in lobby.

_____ Place any added theme accessories in rest rooms.

_____ Have favors, press kits, or other giveaways ready for distribution.

ON THE DAY OF THE PARTY

_____ Have guest list, media list, name tags, and/or table assignments alphabetized and ready at the door.

_____ Set out table numbers and place cards on tables according to charts.

_____ Post staff members to personally escort guests inside.

_____ If needed, place directional signs in lobby.

_____ Place any added theme accessories in rest rooms.

_____ Have favors, press kits, or other giveaways ready for distribution.

PARTY FOLLOW-UP

_____ Pay bills.

_____ Plant gossip column items or send follow-up releases where appropriate.

_____ Write thank-you notes. Send flowers or gifts to those who made a special contribution.

Walk-Through Checklist

Once, soon after you've selected your party site, then again a week before the party, physically inspect your space to make sure it is absolutely ready to receive your guests.

GETTING TO THE PARTY SPACE

_____ If there are parking facilities, are they clearly marked as guests arrive and lit for guests leaving the party?

_____ If transportation is being provided, are guests clear on where it will be waiting?

_____ Is the location of the party clearly indicated when guests enter the building?

_____ Is the elevator service adequate to carry your guests without long waits? If not, can it be improved for the hours when guests are arriving?

_____ Is the elevator attractive? Can it be given a festive touch in keeping with the party?

_____ Who will greet guests when they emerge from the elevator?

_____ Is there a convenient table set aside where guests check in and receive name tags and/or seat assignments?

_____ Is the coat check in a location where it will not cause a traffic jam?

_____ Is there room for briefcases and umbrellas in the check room?

_____ Is there enough coat check staff to avoid long lines?

_____ Are staff members appointed to bring guests inside and make a few introductions?

DURING THE PARTY

_____ If a reception line will be used, where will it be placed?

_____ Is someone appointed to direct each person in the line to the correct location?

_____ Does the placement of food and bars make for easy traffic flow? (Do trial runs with the caterer or planner as though you were a guest to be sure no bottlenecks exist.)

_____ Are all necessary hors d'oeuvre toothpicks, napkins, matches, etc., on hand?

_____ Have you discussed with the caterer how often waiters will circulate with trays of food?

_____ Do guests have a place to put down dirty glasses and plates? Check who will take them away and how often.

_____ If there is a buffet, have you appointed someone to start the line? Guests may be reluctant to be first.

_____ Are table numbers or identifying signs ready?

_____ Will rest rooms be equipped with paper, soap, tissue, and towels? (If there is a party theme or color scheme, it is a nice touch to carry it into the rest rooms.)

_____ Will rest room floors be freshly cleaned the day of the party?

_____ Are there enough ashtrays for smokers?

_____ To avoid guests lingering too long, have you given caterers a time for closing the bar and stopping food service?

_____ Do all microphones and lights work properly? *Test them!*

Resource List

THE LISTING that follows is a selection of party planners and caterers most highly recommended by local sources in major cities in the United States and Canada. Use it as a starting point for your own research (and follow the suggestions on page 7 to expand your list further). The key below indicates which functions each of the listed individuals and firms will perform; some prepare food only, some specialize solely in design, others will supervise all aspects of the event. Also included are recommendations for florists and for special party spaces in each city.

PP = Party planner—plans events, hires all other professionals, including caterers and party designers, and coordinates their efforts.
PD = Party designer—specializes in setting, decor, and lighting.
FC = Full-service caterer—party planning and coordination as well as food preparation.
C = Caterer—food preparation only.

ATLANTA

Party Professionals

AFFAIRS TO REMEMBER
680 Ponce de Leon Ave.
Atlanta, GA 30308
(404)872-7859 **(FC)**

THE ART OF COOKING
1475 Terrell Mill Rd.
Marietta, GA 30667
(404)952-3992 **(FC)**

DELECTABLES
1 Margaret Mitchell Sq.
Atlanta, GA 30303
(404)681-2909 **(FC)**

PRESENTING ATLANTA
110 E. Andrews Dr. NW, Suite 301
Atlanta, GA 30305
(404)231-0200 **(PP)**

PROOF OF THE PUDDING
980 Piedmont Ave.
Atlanta, GA 30309
(404)892-2359 **(FC)**
(Exclusive caterer for Carter Presidential Center)

MURPHY'S CATERING
(and Restaurant)
1019 Los Angeles Ave.
Atlanta, GA 30306
(404)872-6992 **(C)**

TOUGHY'S EATABLES
524 E. Paces Ferry Rd.
Atlanta, GA 30305
(404)233-5451 **(FC)**

TUXEDO CATERING
710 Peachtree St. NE
Atlanta, GA 30308
(404)872-1350 **(FC)**

Florists

FLOWER LADY
3211 Cains Hill Pl. NW
Atlanta, GA 30305
(404)261-3551

GLORIOUS EVENTS
Box 7986B
Atlanta, GA 30309
(404)524-6865

GRIGGS, VAN HORN
200 Arizona Ave. NE
Atlanta, GA 30307
(404)371-1071

MARVIN GARDENS
99 W. Paces Ferry Rd. NW
Atlanta, GA 30305
(404)231-1988

ROBBS FLOWERS OF THE FIELD
793 Peachtree St.
Atlanta, GA 30308
(404)875-9535

Party Spaces

ACADEMY OF MEDICINE
Elegant classical foyer with chandelier, used in *Gone with the Wind*
(404)881-1714

APPAREL MART ATRIUM
7-story atrium with waterfall
(404)681-1222

ATLANTA BOTANICAL GARDENS
(404)876-5858

ATLANTA WOMEN'S CLUB
Granite mansion
(404)237-4849

CALLANWOLDE
Restored Southern mansion
(404)872-5338

CARTER PRESIDENTIAL CENTER
New, contemporary
(404)420-5100

CYCLORAMA
Room surrounded by giant panorama of the Battle of Atlanta
(404)658-6374

FOX THEATRE
Restored Moorish theater with Egyptian ballroom
(404)377-2400

GOLDEN KEY HONOR SOCIETY
Restored historic home
(404)377-2400

GRANT PARK ZOO
(404)658-6374

HIGH MUSEUM OF ART
(404)892-3600

NEW GEORGIA RAILROAD
75-year-old steam engine train that travels 18-mile loop around the city
(404)656-0769

OLD TRAIN DEPOT
Restored 1869 station
(404)656-3850

RHODES HALL
Elaborate historic home owned by Georgia Trust for Historic Preservation
(404)881-9980

ROBERT W. WOODRUFF ARTS CENTER GALLERIA
(Adjacent to High Museum)
(404)892-3600

STONE MOUNTAIN PARK
For barbeques, riverboat rides
(404)498-5600

TWIN TOWERS ATRIUM
4-story atrium facing the state
capitol building
(404)656-3850

BOSTON

Party Professionals

THE CATERED AFFAIR
333 Gannett Rd. N.
Scituate, MA 02066
(617)545-4670 **(FC)**

CREATIVE CELEBRATIONS
93 Beacon St.
Somerville, MA 02143
(617)497-2009 **(FC)**

CREATIVE GOURMETS LTD.
31 Antwerp St.
Boston, MA 02135
(617)242-7676 **(FC)**

DEBRA'S CATERING TO YOUR EVERY WHIM, INC.
841 Beacon St.
Newton, MA 02159
(617)969-4666 **(FC)**

PERFECT SURROUNDINGS
Richard Carbotti
79 Thames St.
Newport, RI 03840
(401)849-1320 **(PD)**

REBECCA'S
21 Charles St.
Boston, MA 02114
(617)742-9747 **(C)**

SEASONS AND OCCASIONS
8 Garden Ct.
Somerville, MA 02143
(617)666-3515 **(FC)**

SIDELL & SASSE
40 Court St.
Boston, MA 02108
(617)277-6565 **(FC)**

UNCOMMON BOSTON
437 Boylston St.
Boston, MA 02116
(617)731-5854 **(PP)**

Florists

BON VIVANT
443 Albany St.
Boston, MA 02110
(617)439-7999

DAVID KIRKBRIDE
589 Tremont St.
Boston, MA 02118
(617)267-2801

DUTCH FLOWER GARDEN
40 Brattle St.
Cambridge, MA 02138
(617)491-0660

FLORAL ARTISTRY
Box 1603
Manchester by the Sea, MA 01944
(617)526-4159

FOXGLOVE
443 Albany St.
Boston, MA 02116
(617)426-3643

HARBOR GREENERY
117 Atlantic Ave.
Boston, MA 02110
(617)523-6131
and
66 School St.
Boston, MA 02119
(617)523-8420

PLANTAE
Westin Hotel
10 Huntington Ave.
Boston, MA 02117
(617)437-7799

STAPLETON FLORISTS
635 East Broadway St.
South Boston, MA 02127
(617)269-7271

TOMMY'S
450 Harrison Ave.
Boston, MA 02118
(617)350-0221

VICTORIAN BOUQUET
53 Charles St.
Boston, MA 02114
(617)367-6648

WINSTON
131 Newberry St.
Boston, MA 02116
(617)536-6861

Party Spaces

AMBIANCE
Yacht rental
(617)265-0729

BALLROOM, BOSTON CENTER FOR ADULT EDUCATION
Edwardian ballroom with
fireplace
(617)267-2465

BOSTON HARBOR CRUISES
(617)227-4320

BOSTON TEA PARTY SHIP
Replica of the original moored
in Boston Harbor
(617)338-1773

CASTLE HILL
Mansion on 165 acres
overlooking the sea
(617)356-4351

THE CHILDREN'S MUSEUM
Innovative exhibits
(617)426-6500

THE COMPUTER MUSEUM
Only one of its kind in the U.S.
(617)426-2800

CRANE ESTATE, IPSWICH
Water views
(508)356-4354

DE CORDOVA & DANA MUSEUM AND PARK
Castlelike building with terrace
on 35 acres
(617)259-8355

THE DOME AND THE GREAT HALL
Faneuil Hall Marketplace
(617)742-2070

INSTITUTION OF CONTEMPORARY ART
Modern art in a 19th-century
police station
(617)266-5151

ISABELLA STEWART GARDNER MUSEUM
Venetian palazzo
(617)734-1359

JOHN F. KENNEDY LIBRARY
Striking glassed pavilion
overlooking the bay
(617)929-4552

MUSEUM OF FINE ARTS
(617)267-9300

MUSEUM OF SCIENCE
(617)723-2500

NEW ENGLAND AQUARIUM
(617)742-8830

SKY WALK AT PRUDENTIAL TOWER
360-degree city views from
50th floor
(617)236-3318

SUMMIT ROOM, JOHN HANCOCK OBSERVATORY
Top views from city's tallest
building
(617)421-5179

CHICAGO

Party Professionals

CALIHAN-GOTOFF
942 W. Huron St.
Chicago, IL 60622
(312)829-4644 **(FC)**

CALVIN REEVES CUISINE
1921 W. North Ave.
Chicago, IL 60622
(312)292-0022 **(C)**

CHICAGO CATERERS
2901 W. Ashland
Chicago, IL 60657
(312)975-8400 **(FC)**

EVENTS ALIVE
(Does marketing and PR as well
 as event planning)
1350 N. Wells St.
Chicago, IL 60610
(312)943-7795 **(PP)**

FERREE-FLORSHEIM
6500 W. Dakin St.
Chicago, IL 60630
(312)282-6100 **(FC)**

GEORGE L. JEWELL SERVICES
110 W. Belmont St.
Chicago, IL 60657
(312)935-6316 **(FC)**

MARIANNE CRUIKSHANK
1500 Lake Shore Dr.
Chicago, IL 60610
(312)951-0777 **(PP)**

ZARADA GOWENLOCK
(Food consultant)
666 N. Lake Shore Dr.
Chicago, IL 60611
(312)337-3337 **(PP)**

Florists

BLOSSOMS
112 Cress Creek Sq.
Naperville, IL 60540
(312)357-5235

CAROL'S BEAUTIFUL FLOWERS
717 Elm St.
Winnetka, IL 60093
(312)446-7700

CREST FINE FLOWERS
417½ Fourth St.
Wilmette, IL 60091
(312)273-2282

DESIGNS BY JODY
13110 W. Highway 176
Lake Bluff, IL 60044
(312)234-0625

FLORAL DESIGNS
3021 N. Southport
Chicago, IL 60657-4278
(312)528-9800

JASON RICHARDS
363 W. Chicago Ave.
Chicago, IL 60610
(312)664-0605

RONSLEY, INC.
363 W. Ontario
Chicago, IL 60610
(312)427-1948

VIRGINIA WOLFF
1332 W. Lake St.
Chicago, IL 60607
(312)226-1777

Party Spaces

ART INSTITUTE OF CHICAGO
(312)443-3530

CHICAGO FROM THE LAKE
200-passenger cruise boat
(312)922-4020

CHICAGO PUBLIC LIBRARY CULTURAL CENTER
(312)269-2900

DEWES MANSION
(312)477-3075

FIELD MUSEUM OF NATURAL HISTORY
(312)922-9410

NAVY PIER
Landmark with domed
 ballroom on Lake Michigan
(312)744-4219

RIALTO SQUARE THEATRE, JOLIET
Magnificently restored 1926
 theater
(815)725-7171

SHEDD AQUARIUM
(312)939-2426

S.S. CLIPPER
361-foot luxury liner
(312)329-1800

TERRA MUSEUM OF AMERICAN ART
(312)664-3939

CLEVELAND

Party Professionals

BRADLEY CATERERS
26001 Mailes Rd.
Cleveland, OH 44128
(216)292-4530 **(FC)**

EDIBLE ARTS, INC.
12277 W. Sixth St.
Cleveland, OH 44113
(216)863-6293 **(FC)**

EXECUTIVE ARRANGEMENTS
13221 Shaker Sq.
Cleveland, OH 44120
(216)991-8333 **(PP)**

EXECUTIVE CATERERS
2101 Lander Rd.
Cleveland, OH 44124
(216)449-0700 **(FC)**

HOUGH CATERING & BAKERY
1519 Lakeview Rd.
Cleveland, OH 44112
(216)795-0600 **(FC)**

NORTH COAST TOURS, INC.
601 Rockeville St. #418
Cleveland, OH 44114
(216)579-6161 **(PP)**

SIMPLY ELEGANT
2536 Miles Rd.
Bedford Heights, OH 44146
(216)464-4044 **(FC)**

Florists

DON VANDERBROOK
3113 Mayfield Rd.
Cleveland, OH 44118
(216)371-0164

GREVE'S FLOWERS
2270 Lee Rd.
Cleveland, OH 44118
(216)932-8855

PALERMO FLORIST & FLORAL DECORATORS
4615 Mayfield Rd.
Cleveland, OH 44121
(216)381-8050

Party Spaces

CLEVELAND ARCADE
1890 Victorian shopping
 complex, historic landmark
(216)621-8500

CLEVELAND MUSEUM OF ART
(216)421-7340

CRAWFORD AUTO AND AVIATION MUSEUM
(216)721-5722

GALLERIA SHOPPING COMPLEX
(216)621-5722

GOODTIME II
Boat charter service
(216)861-5110
(Winter, (216)257-1411)

HALLE BUILDING
Marble lobby with brass and
fountain
(216)523-2243

NATURAL HISTORY
MUSEUM
Courtyard in center
(216)231-4600

TROLLEY TOURS OF
CLEVELAND
(216)771-4484

DALLAS

Party Professionals

AN AFFAIR TO
REMEMBER
4225 W. Lover's Lane
Dallas, TX 75209
(214)357-0013-5401 **(PP)**

CARR'S CATERING
4950 Keller Springs Rd.,
Suite 340
Addison, TX 75248
(214)490-4384 **(FC)**

CYNTHIA MICHAELS
CATERING
(Has its own soundstage facility
for special events)
11106 N. Stemmons Frwy.
Dallas, TX 75229
(214)243-1038 **(FC)**

DALLAS EPICURE INC.
2156 W. Northwest Hwy.,
Suite 312
Dallas, TX 75220
(214)556-0660 **(FC)**

FOOD COMPANY
215 Henry St.
Dallas, TX 75226
(214)939-9270 **(FC)**

Florists

FLOWERS ON THE
SQUARE
311 Main St.
Ft. Worth, TX 76102
(817)429-2888

POTTED PALM
2707 Fairmont
Dallas, TX 75201
(214)871-1055

ZEN
3526 Cedar Springs Rd.
Dallas, TX 75219
(214)526-9736

Party Spaces

DALLAS ART MUSEUM
(214)922-9857

DALLAS ZOO
(214)946-5154

DE GOLYER ESTATE AND
CAMP HOUSE IN THE
ARBORETUM
(214)327-8265

HALL OF STATES AT
FAIR PARK
Art Deco Great Hall with Texas
murals
(214)421-5136

SOUTH FORK RANCH,
PLANO
Site of "Dallas" filming
(214)442-6536

SOUTHWEST MUSEUM
OF SCIENCE AND
HISTORY
(214)428-7200

DENVER

Party Professionals

ATMOSPHERE—FAY
GARDENSCHWARTZ
6425 N. Washington St.,
Unit 12
Denver, CO 80229
(303)759-5297 **(PP)**

EPICUREAN
469 S. Cherry St.,
Suite 120
Denver, CO 80222
(303)321-0343 **(FC)**

FOOTER'S
700 Lincoln
Denver, CO 80218
(303)893-1222 **(FC)**

GREENWOOD CATERERS
7925 E. Harvard, #G
Denver, CO 80231
(303)695-6666 **(FC)**

PANACHE
1579 S. Pearl St.
Denver, CO 80210
(303)777-9260 **(FC)**

LE PETIT GOURMET
4182 E. Virginia Ave.
Denver, CO 80222
(303)388-5791 **(FC)**

Florists

BOUQUETS
2908 E. Sixth St.
Denver, CO 80206
(303)333-5500

D'CLEMENT CUSTOM
FLORIST
4500 Leetsdale Dr.
Denver, CO 80222
(303)399-5543

LOOP FLORIST
1510 California
Denver, CO 80202
(303)629-1717

MICHAEL JULTECK
5151 E. Colfax Ave.
Denver, CO 80220
(303)388-6411

REYBURN-DAVIS
215 St. Paul
Denver, CO 80206
(303)394-3311

Party Spaces

ATRIUM OF TUSCANY
BUILDING
4-story-high building top with
mountain views
(303)771-0449

CASTLE PINES GOLF
CLUB
(303)688-6000

DENVER DESIGN
CENTER
Striking use of marble and glass
(303)733-2455

DENVER MUSEUM OF
NATURAL HISTORY
(303)370-6309

MAMMOTH EVENT
CENTER
Large open space good for
themes
(303)860-1333

MUSEUM OF WESTERN
ART
(303)296-1880

OUTPOST
Square-dance hall
(303)755-0377

PARKSIDE SUITES
Handsome restoration
(303)394-3672

PHIPPS MANSION
Lovely Georgian home
(303)777-4441

TOP OF REPUBLIC
PLAZA BUILDING
Views from the 55th floor
(303)592-5005

HOUSTON

Party Professionals

THE ACUTE CATERING COMPANY
2001 Halcombe Blvd.,
  Suite 2605
Houston, TX 77030
(713)795-4633 **(FC)**

FLINGS AND THINGS
Kay Herrington
P.O. Box 980095
Houston, TX 77098
(713)520-8022 **(PP)**

JACKSON & COMPANY
P.O. Box 130260
River Oaks Sta.
Houston, TX 77219
(713)523-5780 **(FC)**

KIRK SCHLEIN
1141 E. 11th St.
Houston, TX 77009
(713)861-6769 **(FC)**

MARTHANN MASTERSON
714 W. Alabama
Houston, TX 77006
(713)522-1510 **(FC)**

RICK BIEHL
1981 Welch
Houston, TX 77019
(713)524-2094 **(FC)**

SHARON GRAHAM
8775 S. Gessner
Houston, TX 77074
(713)526-0793 **(C)**

Florists

BRENT SAUNDERS— SPECIAL ARRANGEMENTS
1325 Campbell Rd.
Houston, TX 77055
(713)932-9000

CUT FLOWERS
2503 Rice Blvd.
Houston, TX 77005
(713)521-9653

DAVID BROWN
2625 Colquitt
Houston, TX 77098
(713)521-1191

LEONARD THARP
2705 Bammel Lane
Houston, TX 77095
(713)527-9393

MICHAEL DUERR
427 Columbia
Houston, TX 77007
(713)869-8511

ROOTS, INC.
5250 Gulfton
Houston, TX 77081
(713)667-1718

Party Spaces

THE GOODYEAR BLIMP
(713)353-2401

HOUSTON STUDIOS
Sound stage ideal for transformations
(713)223-0951

INNOVA HOUSTON
Award-winning ultra-modern design center
(713)963-9955

MAGNOLIA BALLROOM
(713)223-8508

MUSEUM OF FINE ARTS
Mies van der Rohe design
(713)526-1361

REPUBLIC BANK BUILDING
Available for charity events only
(713)224-0181

WORTHEIM THEATRE
Restored landmark
(713)237-1439

LOS ANGELES

Party Professionals

ALONG CAME MARY
5265 W. Bico Blvd.
Los Angeles, CA 90019
(213)931-9082 **(PP, FC)**

AMBROSIA CATERING
13420 Zanja St.
Venice, CA 90291
(213)392-8547 **(C)**

BRIER-KUSHNER ASSOCIATES
1104 S. Robertson Blvd.
Los Angeles, CA 90005
(213)274-8819 **(PP)**

CALIFORNIA CELEBRATIONS
4051 Glencoe Ave.,
  Suite 7
Los Angeles, CA 90292
(213)305-8849 **(FC)**

DUCK DUCK MOUSSE
5714½ W. Pico Blvd.
Los Angeles, CA 90019
(213)930-1344 **(FC)**

L.A. CELEBRATIONS
1716 S. Robertson Blvd.
Los Angeles, CA 90035
(213)837-8900 **(FC)**

MICHAELS, RUBIN & ASSOCIATES— SPECIAL EVENTS
2901 Wilshire Blvd., Suite 441
Santa Monica, CA 90403
(213)829-7496 **(PP)**

PARTIES PLUS, INC.
3455 S. La Cienega Blvd.
Los Angeles, CA 90016
(213)838-3800 **(PP, FC)**

PARTY PLANNERS WEST, INC.
8761 Venice Blvd.
Los Angeles, CA 90034
(213)838-2100 **(PP)**

ROCOCO CUSTOM CATERING SERVICE
6734 Valjean Ave.
Van Nuys, CA 91406
(818)909-0990 **(FC)**

Florists

HEAP O' FLOWERS
661 N. Spaulding Ave.
Los Angeles, CA 90036
(213)653-6923

JOHN DALY
2210 Wilshire Blvd.
Santa Monica, CA 90403
(213)828-1179

NATURE'S WAY OF GIVING
12208 Darlington Ave.
Los Angeles, CA 90049
(213)826-3216

SECRET GARDEN— DAVID YEH
221 S. Robertson Blvd.
Beverly Hills, CA 90211
(213)659-5854

Party Spaces

CATALINA SAFARI
Trips to Catalina Island for picnics
(213)510-0303

DOROTHY CHANDLER PAVILION
Grand hall and/or plaza
(213)972-7478

GREEK THEATRE
Griffith Park
(213)665-6887

HOLLYHOCK HOUSE
Home designed by Frank Lloyd Wright
(213)485-4580

KASTEEL KAMPHUYZEN
Dutch castle in Beverly Hills
(213)276-5191

R.M.S. *QUEEN MARY*
(213)435-3511

**TWENTIETH CENTURY-
FOX STUDIOS**
Choice of movie sets
(213)277-2211

UNIVERSAL STUDIOS
More movie sets
(818)777-3950

WILTERN THEATRE
Restored Art Deco landmark
(213)388-1400

Specialist in unusual
L.A. party locations:

**MARILYN JENETT
LOCATIONS**
2 Century Plaza,
Suite 1200
2049 Century Park E.
Los Angeles, CA 90067
(213)551-1488

MIAMI

Party Professionals

(As a major convention city,
Miami has many party
planners.)

BILL'S CATERING
1 SE Third Ave.
Miami, FL 33131
(305)374-7300 **(FC)**

**CULINARY
COMMUNICATIONS—
MARINA POLVAY**
1175 NE 125th Street, Suite 503
North Miami, FL 33161
(305)892-8307 **(PP)**

DETAILS, DETAILS
6816 Camarin
Coral Gables, FL 33146
(305)665-4380 **(PP)**

**EXECUTIVE SOCIAL
PLANNER**
5445 Collins Ave.
Miami Beach, FL 33141
(305)864-9747 **(PP)**

GENE SINGLETARY
8944 NW 24th Terr.
Miami, FL 33172
(305)592-1311 **(FC)**

JAMES LAWSON DESIGN
6400 NE Four Court
Miami, FL 33138
(305)757-0502 **(PP)**

THE MAIN EVENT
2194 NW 89th Pl.
Miami, FL 32172
(305)594-1904 **(PP)**

**PARTIES BY NEIL AND
ENTERTAINMENT, ETC.**
2329 SW 31st Ave.
Hallandale, FL 33009
(305)374-1505 **(PP)**

SARA SHARPE
4209 Salzedo
Coral Gables, FL 33146
(305)443-4399 **(FC)**

SENTER AND CHESS
7399 SW 45th St.
Miami, Fl 33155
(305)442-6815 **(FC)**

Florists

ANNE NOVELLI
4812 SW 72nd Ave
Miami, FL 33155
(305)665-4022

CYPRESS GARDEN
10691 Sunset Dr.
Miami, FL 33173
(305)595-6336

JENNY'S
6807 Biscayne Blvd.
Miami, FL 33138
(305)758-5553

**JILL ADDA, FLORAL
DESIGN ASSOCIATES**
3028 NW 72nd Ave.
Miami, FL 33122
(305)477-2303

LIVING THINGS
456 41st St.
Miami Beach, FL 33140
(305)673-2994

**REBECCA SNYDER
AT LOUIE'S
FLOWER GALLERY**
1071 Kane Concourse
Bay Harbor Island
Miami Beach, FL 33154
(305)868-5600

STAR FLORIST
2221 SW 27th Ave.
Miami, FL 33142
(305)856-5000

Party Spaces

**FLAGLER GREYHOUND
TRACK**
(305)649-3000

GULF STREAM PARK
(305)940-5085

HIALEAH RACE TRACK
(305)885-8000

JOHN DEERING ESTATE
Elaborate home and grounds
(305)255-4767

**JOHN LLOYD STATE
PARK, DANIA**
For picnic outings
(305)923-2833

LOWE ART MUSEUM
University of Miami, Coral
Gables
(305)284-3535

**METRO-DADE CULTURAL
CENTER PLAZA**
Showplace Philip Johnson–
designed plaza surrounded by
city museums and library.
Phone Center for the Fine Arts
for information.
(305)375-1700

METROZOO
(305)251-0401

MIAMI SEAQUARIUM
(305)361-5703

VIZCAYA
Venetian villa on the bay
(305)579-2708

YACHT RENTALS
Florida Yacht Charter
(305)672-8922
or
Sailaway Yacht Rental
(305)577-3355

MINNEAPOLIS–ST. PAUL

Party Professionals

CHRISTIAN CATERING
2451 Hennepin Ave.
Minneapolis, MN 55405
(612)377-1759 **(FC)**

CHUCKWAGON
(Specializes in outdoor
barbecues)
3105 Shores Blvd.
Minnetonka, MN 55345
(612)473-7041 **(C)**

LE PETIT CHEF
5932 Excelsior Blvd.
St. Louis Park, MN 55416
(612)926-9331 **(FC)**

PROM CATERING
(Known for large functions)
1190 University Ave.
St. Paul, MN 55104
(612)645-0596 **(FC)**

QUAIL CATERING
1837 E. 38th St.
Minneapolis, MN 55407
(612)722-2780 **(FC)**

SUZANNE'S CUISINE
4701 Clark Ave.
White Bear Lake, MN 55110
(612)426-8999 **(FC)**

TOWN AND COUNTRY
301A Broadway Ave.
Wayzata, MN 55391
(612)473-5441 **(FC)**

TROVARE CATERING
1 E. Little Canada Rd.
St. Paul, MN 55107
(612)483-1805 **(FC)**

WATSON'S CENTER CUISINE
2240 North Shore Dr.
Wayzata, MN 55391
(612)476-2208 **(FC)**

Florists

BUTTERFIELDS ON THE MALL
1300 Nicollet Mall
Minneapolis, MN 55403
(612)332-2979

JERRY PALMER
2737 Winnetka Ave. N.
Minneapolis, MN 55427
(612)545-5637

MINNEAPOLIS FLORAL
2420 Hennepin Ave. S.
Minneapolis, MN 55405
(612)377-8080

SALISBURY FLOWER MARKET, INC.
219 SE Main St.
Minneapolis, MN 55414
(612)623-1196

SCHAAF FLORAL
6554 University Ave., NE
Minneapolis, MN 55432
(612)571-4600

Party Spaces

BROWN RYAN BANQUET FACILITIES
Refurbished stable
(612)378-0154

COMO PARK CONSERVATORY, ST. PAUL
Set amid park and gardens
(612)489-1740

EDINBOROUGH PARK, EDINA
New building with attractive
atrium
(612)893-9890

FILLEBROWN HOUSE
Restored mansion
(612)426-0479

FIRST TRUST CENTER, ST. PAUL
Renovation of landmark 1914
building with Great Hall
(612)223-7000

GUTHRIE THEATER
(612)377-2224

INTERNATIONAL MARKET SQUARE
Shopping complex in renovated
factory with 5-story center
atrium
(612)338-6250

LADY OF THE LAKE, INC.
Lake Minnetonka sternwheeler
(612)929-1209

LAKE HARRIET, LAKE CALHOUN AND LAKE OF THE ISLES PARKS
Three of the many city parks
available for outdoor parties
(612)348-2243

LANDMARK CENTER, ST. PAUL
1894 Federal Court Building
(612)292-3225

ORCHESTRA HALL
(612)371-5656

QUEEN OF EXCELSIOR
70-foot party boat
(612)474-2502

RIVER PLACE
Victorian shopping complex
adjoining St. Anthony Main,
also on the river
(612)378-1969

ST. ANTHONY MAIN
Old factory converted into
shopping complex on
Mississippi River
(612)379-4528

WALKER ARTS CENTER
(612)375-7600

NEW ORLEANS

Party Professionals

CAPRICHO
600 Esplanade Ave.
New Orleans, LA 70116
(800)222-7757 **(PP)**

NEW ORLEANS CONNECTIONS
Canal Place I, Suite 2300
New Orleans, LA 70130
(504)527-0047 **(PP)**

LA BONNE BOUCHE
3518 Monticello St.
New Orleans, LA 70118
(504)486-9861 **(FC)**

LARRY HILL CATERERS
221 Royal St.
New Orleans, LA 70130
(504)529-2603 **(FC)**

NEW ORLEANS CATERING
3916 Ford St.
Metairie, LA 70002
(504)454-6802 **(FC)**

PANACHE
1829 Magazine St.
New Orleans, LA 70130
(504)523-1829 **(FC)**

UPPER CRUST
5430 Magazine St.
New Orleans, LA 70115
(504)899-8065 **(FC)**

Florists

F. L. CHOPIN AND SONS FLORIST, INC.
614 S. Carrollton Ave.
New Orleans, LA 70118
(504)861-3686

HARKINS FLORIST
1601 Magazine St.
New Orleans, LA 70130
(504)529-1638

IRWIN'S FLOWER SALON
4238 Magazine St.
New Orleans, LA 70115
(504)897-1313

MAGAZINE FLOWERS
(Exotic flowers)
5501 Magazine St.
New Orleans, LA 70115
(504)891-4356

REBE FLORALS
838 Royal St.
New Orleans, LA 70116
(504)523-1558

ROHM'S
8333 Maple St.
New Orleans, LA 70118
(504)861-3611

Party Spaces

BEAUREGARDE—KEYES HOUSE
1826 historic home with formal
gardens
(504)523-7527

GALLIER HOUSE MUSEUM
Restored 1860s mansion
(504)523-6722

HOUMAS HOUSE PLANTATION, CONVENT
Restored 1800s mansion
(504)522-2262

LONGUE VUE HOUSE AND GARDENS
Grand estate in the city
(504)488-5488

MADEWOOD PLANTATION, NAPOLEONVILLE
1846 historic landmark with
gardens
(504)524-1988

NEW ORLEANS BOTANICAL GARDEN, CITY PARK
(504)482-4888

ENTERTAINING FOR BUSINESS

**NEW ORLEANS
MUSEUM OF ART**
(504)488-2631

**NEW ORLEANS STREET
CAR PARTY**
(504)865-1512

OLD U.S. MINT
National landmark, now a
museum of jazz and Mardi
Gras memorabilia
(504)568-9868

PADDLEWHEELER
CREOLE QUEEN
(504)529-4567

RIVERBOAT *PRESIDENT*
(504)522-3030

NEW YORK CITY

*Party
Professionals*

**ABIGAIL KIRSCH
CULINARY
PRODUCTIONS**
33 Plainfield Ave.
Bedford Hills, NY 10507
(914)666-7545 **(FC)**

BESPOKE FOOD
311 East 81st St.
New York, NY 10028
(212)794-2248 **(FC)**

**CAPRICHO SPECIAL
EVENTS**
4 East 10th St.
New York, NY 10003
(800)222-7757 **(PP)**

**CULINARY
PRODUCTIONS**
237 Third Ave.
New York, NY
(212)598-4890 **(FC)**

DAVID LEES DESIGN
807 Ave. of the Americas
New York, NY 10001
(212)888-7406 **(PD)**

THE EVENT GROUP
67 East 11th St.,
Suite 509
New York, NY 10003
(212)529-3639 **(FC)**

FOOD GALLERY
219 West 29th St.
New York, NY 10001
(212)594-7701 **(FC)**

FRED ROTHBERG
193 Baltica St.
Brooklyn, NY 11201
(718)852-3673 **(C)**

GARNET WILLIAMSON
424 East 52nd St.
New York, NY 10022
(212)935-6366 **(PP, FC)**

GEORGE PRIFTY
265 Water St.
New York, NY 10038
(212)513-7550 **(C)**

GLORIOUS FOODS
172 East 75th St.
New York, NY 10021
(212)628-2320 **(C)**

GOLDEN PHEASANT
(Specializes in Italian country
cuisine)
Kings Highway
Sugar Loaf, NY 10981
(914)469-7474 **(C)**

GREAT PERFORMANCES
125 Crosby St.
New York, NY 10012
(212)219-2800 **(FC)**

**JOSEPH BAUM AND
MICHAEL WHITEMAN
SPECIAL EVENTS
PLANNERS, INC.**
186 Fifth Ave.
New York, NY 10010
(212)206-7114 **(PP, FC)**

KARIN BACON EVENTS
349 West End Ave.,
4th floor
New York, NY 10024
(212)724-3687 **(PP)**

LAVIN CATERING
23 West 39th St.
New York, NY 10018
(212)944-0101 **(C)**

MARK FAHRER
43 West 13th St.
New York, NY 10011
(212)243-6572 **(FC)**

**McNABB AND
ASSOCIATES**
121 West 27th St.,
Suite 604
New York, NY 10001
(212)989-7877 **(PD)**

MICHAEL ERESHENA
557 Third St.
Brooklyn, NY 11215
(718)965-1625 **(PD)**

MOVEABLE FEAST
71 West End Avenue
Brooklyn, NY 11235
(718)891-3999 **(C)**

NEW YORK PARTIES
22 East 13th St.
New York, NY 10003
(212)777-3565 **(FC)**

NICHOLAS BAXTER
692 Greenwich St.
New York, NY 10014
(212)463-0001 **(FC)**

PEGGY MULHOLLAND
245 East 37th St.
New York, NY 10016
(212)953-9105 **(PP)**

**PERFECT PARTY
PLANNING**
166 East 61st St.
New York, NY 10021
(212)753-1002 **(FC)**

**PHILIP BALOUN
DESIGNS**
340 West 55th St.
New York, NY 10019
(212)307-1675 **(PD)**

PROJECTS PLUS
(Fund-raising event specialists)
1500 Broadway
(212)997-0100 **(PP)**

REMEMBER BASIL
11 Cadman Plaza
Brooklyn, NY 11201
(718)858-3000 **(C)**

**RENNY DESIGN FOR
ENTERTAINING**
159 East 64th St.
New York, NY 10021
(212)228-7000 **(PD)**

**RESTAURANT
ASSOCIATE
CATERERS**
36 West 44th St.
New York, NY 10036
(212) 642-1546 **(FC)**

ROBERT ISABELL
89 Jane St.
New York, NY 10014
(212)645-7767 **(PD)**

**SARA FOSTER
CELEBRATIONS**
374½ Greenwich Ave.
Greenwich, CT 06830
(203)869-9545 **(FC)**

**SINGER &
ENGELHARDT, INC.**
(Fund-raising event specialists)
1841 Broadway,
Suite 1008
New York, NY 10023
(212)586-2820 **(PP)**

SPECIAL ATTENTION
333 East 30th Street
New York, NY 10016
(212)683-6569 **(FC)**

TASTE CATERERS, INC.
151 Hudson St.
New York, NY 10013
(212)929-5074 **(FC)**

WOK ON WHEELS
(Chinese cuisine)
306 East 15th St.
New York, NY 10003
(212)777-3420 **(C)**

Florists

FRESH ART
77 Irving Pl.
New York, NY 10003
(212)288-7000

MADDERLAKE LTD.
25 East 73rd St.
New York, NY 10021
(212)879-8400

MARLO FLOWERS LIMITED
421 East 73rd St.
New York, NY 10021
(212)628-2246

PRESTON BAILEY FELLAN COMPANY
192 East 72nd St.
New York, NY 10021
(212)288-7848

RENNY
159 East 64th St.
New York, NY 10021
(212)288-7000

RICHARD SALONE
152 East 79th St.
New York, NY 10021
(212)988-2933

RONALDO MAIA LTD.
27 East 67th St.
New York, NY 10021
(212)288-1049

SALOU
452A Columbus Ave.
New York, NY 10024
(212)595-9604

SURROUNDINGS
2295 Broadway
New York, NY 10024
(212)580-8982

TWIGS, INC.
399 Bleecker St.
New York, NY 10014
(212)620-8188

VERY SPECIAL FLOWERS
215 West 10th St.
New York, NY 10014
(212)206-7236

YORK FLORAL COMPANY, INC.
104 West 27th Street
New York, NY 10001
(212)627-1840

Party Spaces

ABIGAIL ADAMS SMITH MUSEUM
18th-century mansion with garden
(212)838-7225

AMERICAN CRAFT MUSEUM
(212)956-3535

AMERICAN MUSEUM OF NATURAL HISTORY
(212)873-6380

THE BALLROOM AT WINDOWS ON THE WORLD
Views from the city's tallest building
(212)938-0032

BARGEMUSIC
Floating concert hall in Brooklyn, breathtaking Manhattan views
(718)624-4061

THE DAIRY AND THE BOATHOUSE, CENTRAL PARK
(212)397-3156

ENID A. HAUPT CONSERVATORY, NEW YORK BOTANICAL GARDEN
(212)220-8773

FEDERAL HALL
Columned Wall Street landmark, first federal capitol
(212)264-8854

JAMES BEARD HOUSE
The late culinary authority's Greenwich Village town house and garden
(212)675-4984

LA BELLE EPOQUE
Ballroom in the grand French manner
(212)254-6436

MORRIS-JUMEL MANSION
Manhattan's oldest residence
(212)923-8008

NATIONAL ACADEMY OF DESIGN
Old World mansion with grand staircase
(212)369-4880

PIER 17, SOUTH STREET SEAPORT
Glass-enclosed atrium on the river; bridge and Statue of Liberty views
(212)732-7678

PUCK BUILDING
Turn-of-the-century landmark
(212)226-0603

RAINBOW ROOM
Art Deco beauty atop Rockefeller Center
(212)757-9090

RIVER BOATS AT SOUTH STREET: *DeWITT CLINTON*, *ANDREW FLETCHER*
(212)406-3434

ROSELAND BALLROOM
Recently redesigned vintage dance palace
(212)247-0200

THE TERRACE
Traditional elegance, wraparound windows with river views
(212)666-9490

WHITNEY MUSEUM OF AMERICAN ART
(212)570-3600

WORLD YACHT ENTERPRISES
Yacht rentals
(212)627-2775

SCHOONER *FREEDOM*
Tall ship rental
(212)363-5556

STATEN ISLAND FERRY
(212)806-6941

To rent lofts or private town houses in Manhattan, contact Places, (212)737-7536, or see private advertisements under "Party Service" and "Party Space" in *New York* magazine,
(212)880-0700

PHILADELPHIA

Party Professionals

FROG/COMMISSARY CATERING
117 S. 17th St., #2103
Philadelphia, PA 19103
(215)569-2243 **(FC)**

JACK FRANCIS
300 Maple Ave.
Conshohocken, PA 19428
(215)825-0776 **(FC)**

JIMMY DUFFY'S CATERING
1456 Lancaster Ave.
Berwyn, PA 19312
(215)647-0160 **(FC)**

NORMAN FAIR CATERERS
7 New St.
Willow Grove, PA 19090
(215)659-3440 **(FC)**

PIANI'S
(Serves Delaware and
Philadelphia)
2130 N. Market St.
Wilmington, DE 19802
(302)658-4353 **(FC)**

**RAYMOND HOLDERMAN
CATERERS**
110-12 S. Front St.
Philadelphia, PA 19106
(215)925-9888 **(FC)**

**RIDGEWELL'S
CATERERS**
507 S. Second St.
Philadelphia, PA 19147
(215)567-2266 **(FC)**
and
215 W. Church Rd.
King of Prussia, PA 19406
(215)567-2266 **(FC)**

**STREET CORNER
CUISINE**
(Provides pushcarts and venders
with Philly cheese steaks,
pretzels, hot dogs, etc.)
830 Montgomery Ave.,
Suite 215
Bryn Mawr, PA 19010
(215)525-2229 **(C)**

Florists

AMARANTH
134 Lodges Land
Bala Cynwyd, PA 19004
(215)664-1305

CAROUSEL FLOWERS
203 W. State St.
Doylestown, PA 18901
(215)345-4033

**EXOTIC BLOSSOMS
OF PHILADELPHIA**
510 S. Fifth St.
Philadelphia, PA 19147
(215)925-4125

**GEORGE ROBERTSON &
SONS, INC.**
8501 Germantown Ave.
Philadelphia, PA 19118
(215)242-6000,

JAMIE ROTHSTEIN
313 Cherry St.
Philadelphia, PA 19106
(215)238-1220

MOLES' FLORIST
300 W. Ridge Pike
Norristown, PA 19403
(215)631-1660

Party Spaces

ACADEMY OF MUSIC
Mirrored crystal ballroom
(215)893-1935

APPLEFORD
English manor house
(215)527-4280

ATHENEUM LIBRARY
Pillared Victorian room
(215)925-2688

**BEAVER COLLEGE
CASTLE**
(Must have an affiliation)
(215)572-2900

FAIRMOUNT PARK
Horticultural Center, Memorial
Hall, several mansions
(215)879-4062

**FRANKLIN MEMORIAL
HALL, FRANKLIN
INSTITUTE**
(215)448-1165

GRANGE ESTATE
1700s mansion with large
veranda
(215)446-4958

**HILL/PHYSICK/KEITH
HOUSE**
Early Federal mansion
(215)925-7866

**OLD MILL, ROSE
VALLEY**
(215)566-9872

**PENNSYLVANIA
HISTORICAL SOCIETY**
(215)732-6201

**TREEHOUSE AT THE
PHILADELPHIA ZOO**
Charming whimsical indoor
space
(215)879-4062

THE WILLOWS
1910 mansion on 47 acres
(215)527-4280

Party Professionals

**AMERICAN
HOSPITALITY**
1607 63rd St.
Emeryville, CA 94608
(415)653-6699 **(FC)**

BON APPETIT
(Does many large events)
548 Seventh St.
San Francisco, CA 94103
(415)621-4481 **(FC)**

**CAPPA AND GRAHAM,
INC.**
401 China Basin St., Suite 212
San Francisco, CA 94107
(415)542-3484 **(PP)**

**DAN McCALL &
ASSOCIATES**
888 Brannan St.
San Francisco, CA 94103
(415)552-8550 **(FC)**

EDIBLE ART
758 Clementina St.
San Francisco, CA 94103
(415)863-8771 **(FC)**

FRED WERTHEIM
(Exclusive caterer for Duquette
Pavilion)
2150 Third St.
San Francisco, CA 94107
(415)864-0803 **(FC)**

**HOLLANDER &
ASSOCIATES**
3298 Pierce St.
San Francisco, CA 94123
(415)922-1511 **(PP)**

OPT'S CATERING
1455A Market St.,
Suite 408
San Francisco, CA 94103
(415)626-7642 **(FC)**

TASTE CATERERS
55 Rodgers St.
San Francisco, CA 94103
(415)864-4321 **(FC)**

Florists

**ALTERNATIVE
ARRANGEMENTS**
300 Brannan St.
San Francisco, CA 94107
(415)543-6489

BLOOMERS
340 Presidio Ave.
San Francisco, CA 94115
(415)563-3266

**FLOWERS LIMITED—
MICHAEL DAIGIAN**
10 Rogers St.
San Francisco, CA 94103
(415)621-7121

**FLOWERS ON THE HILL
—MICHAEL LABRIE**
47 Powers Ave.
San Francisco, CA 94110
(415)641-4949

LYDIA'S FLOWERS
5 Embarcadero Center
San Francisco, CA 94111
(415)398-6131

**MONTBRETIA—
SYLVIA KOKOLJ**
801 Spring Dr.
Mill Valley, CA 94941
(415)381-2746

Party Spaces

ALCATRAZ ISLAND
(415)556-0575

ASIAN ART MUSEUM
Large courtyard
(415)668-8921

CALIFORNIA PALACE OF THE LEGION OF HONOR
Museum of French culture
(415)221-4811

CONVENT OF THE SACRED HEART
Handsome period building
(415)563-2900

DE YOUNG MUSEUM, HEARST COURT
(415)221-4811

DUQUETTE FOUNDATION, PAVILION OF ST. FRANCIS
(415)864-0803

FLOOD MANSION
(Need Pacific Union Club affiliation)
(415)775-1234

GIFT CENTER PAVILION
Art Deco decor
(415)861-7733

GREEN ROOM IN THE WAR MEMORIAL BUILDING
(415)565-6435

THE OLD MINT BUILDING
(415)974-0788

PALACE OF FINE ARTS
1915 building, noted Exploratorium science exhibits
(415)563-7337

ROUNDABOUT ROOM AT THE AQUARIUM
Fish exhibits all around
(415)221-5100

SAN FRANCISCO OPERA HOUSE
(415)565-6435

SAN FRANCISCO TROLLEY CARS
(415)923-6262

SEATTLE

Party Professionals

THE FAMOUS NORTHWEST CATERING COMPANY AND PACIFIC DESSERTS
420 E. Denny Way
Seattle, WA 98122
(206)328-1950 **(FC)**

GRETCHEN, OF COURSE
1333 Fifth Ave.,
Rainier Square
Seattle, WA 98101
(206)623-8194 **(FC)**

MARKET PLACE CATERERS
3001 E. Yesler Way
Seattle, WA 98122
(206)324-5900 **(FC)**

ROSELLINI'S
2515 Fourth Ave.
Seattle, WA 98121
(206)728-0410 **(FC)**

SEATTLE IN STYLE
93 Pike, Suite 308
Seattle, WA 98101
(206)628-2977 **(PP)**

TINA BELL, THE WEDGE
4760 University Village Pl. NE
Seattle, WA 98105
(206)523-2560 **(FC)**

UPPER CRUST
10900 NE Fourth St.
Bellevue, WA 98004
(206)454-1686 **(FC)**

Florists

MARTHA E. HARRIS
5420 Sand Point Way NE
Seattle, WA 98105
(206)527-1820

MASTER FLORIST
2134 Third Ave.
Seattle, WA 98121
(206)448-ROSE

REDMOND
8070 160th St. NE
Redmond, WA 98051
(206)885-3333

ROBERT HUTCHINSON
Seattle Sheraton Hotel
1400 Sixth Ave.
Seattle, WA 98101
(206)343-7188

TOPPERS
Four Seasons Hotel
411 University
Seattle, WA 98101
(206)622-6330

Party Spaces

CHATEAU STE. MICHELLE AT STE. MICHELLE WINERY
Lovely setting on 47 acres
(206)488-1133

CHINESE ROOM IN SMITH TOWER
Wraparound deck with downtown and water views
(206)682-2939

MUSEUM OF FLIGHT
Striking steel and glass Great Gallery
(206)967-7373

MUSEUM OF HISTORY & INDUSTRY
(206)324-1125

SEATTLE AQUARIUM
(206)628-0860

SEATTLE CENTER
Site of Century 21 World's Fair
(206)625-4234

STIMSON-GREEN MANSION
Restored 1899 Tudor
(206)624-0474

WASHINGTON STATE MUSEUM
(206)543-5590

WOODLAND PARK ZOO
(206)625-4550

WASHINGTON, D.C.

(An excellent guide to Washington caterers and party locations is *Capital Entertaining* by Bunny Pomer and Ann Yonkers, published by 101 Productions, San Francisco.)

Party Professionals

BRAUN'S FINE CATERERS
(Does many large events)
5903 Riggs Rd.
Chillum, MD 20783
(301)559-2400 **(FC)**

CHANTERELLE CATERERS
3714 Macomb St. NW
Washington, DC 20016
(202)363-3900 **(FC)**

DESIGN CUISINE
2828 Dorr Ave.
Fairfax, VA 22031
(703)849-9400 **(FC)**

LANSDOWNE CATERING
2134 Wisconsin Ave. NW
Washington, DC 20007
(202)338-1640 **(FC)**

RIDGEWELL'S CATERER
5525 Dorsy Lane
Bethesda, MD 20816
(301)652-1515 **(FC)**

SALLIE OLMSTED
(Does special events and publicity)
4620 26th St. N.
Arlington, VA 22207
(703)527-2755 **(PP)**

SUE FISCHER AND A COMPANY OF CATERERS
2080 Viers Mill Rd.
Rockville, MD 20851
(301)251-9070 **(C)**

WASHINGTON, INC.
1990 M St. NW,
Suite 310
Washington, DC 20036
(202)828-7000 **(PP)**

Florists

ALAN WOODS
2604 Connecticut Ave. NW
Washington, DC 20008
(202)332-3334

BLUE WILLOW
1729 20th St. NW
Washington, DC 20009
(202)234-9600

NOSEGAY
1120 20th St. NW
Washington, DC 20036
(202)338-1146

WASHINGTON HARBOR FLOWERS BY ANGELO BONITA
3050 K. St. NW,
Suite 145
Washington, DC 20007
(202)944-4600

Party Spaces

ATRIUM, NATIONAL BUILDING MUSEUM
Great Hall is ideal for very large crowds
(202)272-3555

BARGE TRIPS ON THE C & O CANAL
(202)472-4376

CARNEGIE LIBRARY
Fine 19th-century building
(202)282-3007

THE *CHERRY BLOSSOM*
Replica of 19th-century riverboat on the Potomac
(703)684-0580

CORCORAN GALLERY
Elegant Beaux Arts building
(202)638-3211

DECATUR HOUSE
Landmark beauty on Lafayette Square, famed interior maintained by National Trust for Historic Preservation
(202)673-4210

McLEAN GARDENS BALLROOM
Warm decor with fireplaces, perfect for dinner dances
(301)585-9277

MERIDIAN HOUSE INTERNATIONAL
18th-century French architecture
(202)667-6800

NATIONAL PARK SERVICE
Outdoor tents may be put up at the Tidal Basin or Washington Monument Reflecting Pool
(202)426-6690

THE PHILLIPS COLLECTION
Elegant turn-of-the-century home turned gallery
(202)387-2151

SEWALL-BELMONT HOUSE
Federal-style landmark
(202)546-1210

THE TEXTILE MUSEUM
Originally two historic residences
(202)667-0441

THOMAS McKINNON HOUSE
Private mansion with garden in prestigious Kalorama section
(202)234-7069

WASHINGTON BOAT LINES
Potomac River cruises
(202)554-8000

WOODLAWN PLANTATION, MOUNT VERNON, VA
Magnificent 1800s home and gardens
(703)557-7881

National Catering Sources

CAPRICHO
(See headquarters addresses in New York and New Orleans)
(800)222-7757

CAROUSEL INTERNATIONAL CATERING
(Does work all over the country)
10519 Victory Blvd.
North Hollywood, CA 91606
(800)824-8660

PLACES
A Directory of Public Places for Private Events and Private Places for Public Functions
Tenth House Enterprises Inc.
(National Party Location Specialist and Directory Publisher)
Caller Box 810,
Gracie Sta.
New York, NY 10028
(212)737-7536

SPECIAL EVENTS NETWORK
Offers local catering contacts in 38 major cities.
11106 North Stemmons Frwy.
Dallas, TX 75229
(214)243-1038

Party Professionals

AGNUS DEI
Le Faubourg Sainte-Catherine,
#103
1616 ouest, rue Sainte-Catherine
Montreal, PQ, H3H 1L7
(514)937-4216 **(C)**

BROWN DERBY DELICATESSEN
4863, rue Van Horne
Montreal, PQ, H3W 1J2
(514)731-5433 **(C)**

CHANTAL TITTLEY MOREAULT
4315, ave. Girouard
Montreal, PQ, H4A 3E5
(514)481-3302 **(PP)**

GESTION CONGRES
JPDL Conventions-Congres
1410, rue Stanley, bureau 609
Montreal, PQ,
(514)287-1070 **(PP)**

GISELLE GAUTHIER TRAITEUR
4428, blvd. Saint-Laurent
Montreal, PQ,
(514)287-1935 **(C)**

LENOTRE PARIS
1050 ouest, rue Laurier
Montreal, PQ,
(514)270-2702 **(C)**

MARIE-HELENE FOX
Le groupe Columbia
87, ave. Columbia
Montreal, PQ, H3Z 2C4
(514)937-5435 **(PP)**

PIERRE PARENT
Groupe Promexpo
801 est, rue Sherbrooke
Montreal, PQ, H2L 1K6
(514)527-9221 **(PP)**

Florists

THE FLOWER POT
1000 de le Montagne
Montreal, PQ, H3G 1Y7
(514)866-9454

FOLLE AVOINE
5259 St. Laurent
Montreal, PQ H2T 1S4
(514)270-8609

**VAN HORNE
ROBERGE**
1448A Sherbrooke St. W.
Montreal, PQ, H3G 1K9
(514)284-0665

Party Spaces

**ASSOCIATION DES
POURVOYEURS
DU QUEBEC**
Hunting lodges for private
    meetings in rural settings
(514)687-0041

**LE FESTIN DU
GOUVERNEUR
HISTORIC BANQUETS**
Old island fort revives food and
    entertainment of 17th-century
    France
(514)879-1141

OLYMPIC STADIUM
For large-scale events or smaller
    affairs held in top levels
    reached by cable car
(514)252-4646

RITZ-CARLTON HOTEL
Old World charm, garden with
    pond
(514)842-4212

TORONTO

*Party
Professionals*

BRIAN KING
Catering a la Carte
113-115 The Danforth
Toronto, ON, M4K 1N2
(416)463-1101 **(FC)**

CATHIE SZYMCZYK
Project Consultant
668 Windermere Ave.
Toronto, ON, M6S 3M1
(416)762-7249 **(PP)**

DINAH'S CUPBOARD
50 Cumberland St.
Toronto, ON, M4W 1J5
(416) 921-8112 **(C)**

MOVENPICK CATERING
165 York St.
Toronto, ON, M5H 3R8
(416) 366-5234 **(C)**

SHANNON HOWARD
Butler Affairs
233 Manor Road E.
Toronto, ON, M4S 1R9
(416)488-2393 **(PP)**

**WILLIAMS &
ASSOCIATES**
77 Bloor St., Suite 1106
Toronto, ON, M5S 1M2
(416)323-9552 **(PP)**

Florists

BLOSSOMS
One Lowanwood
Toronto, ON, M4W 1Y5
(416)960-8903

COVENT GARDEN
116-B Yonge St.
Toronto, ON, M4W 2L6
(416)960-5800

THE GRAPEVINE
388 Eglinton W.
Toronto, ON, M5N 1A2
(416)488-3212

Party Spaces

**ART GALLERY OF
ONTARIO**
(416)977-0414

CASA LOMA
Medieval-style castle
(416)923-1171

**ENOCH TURNER
SCHOOLHOUSE**
19th-century school
(416)863-0010

**GARDINER MUSEUM OF
CERAMIC ART**
(416)593-9300

MARIPOSA BELLE
Riverboat cruises on the harbor
(416)366-0178

McLEAN HOUSE
In-town estate
(416)487-3841

ROY THOMSON HALL
High-tech concert hall, can take
    both small and large groups
(416)593-4822

**ROYAL ONTARIO
MUSEUM**
(416)586-5571

WARD'S ISLAND
Ferry reaches beach and
    parkland for outdoor
    entertaining
(416)392-8188

**WINDOWS AT THE FOUR
SEASONS HOTEL**
City views from the top
(416)964-0411

VANCOUVER

*Party
Professionals*

**CONTEMPORARY
COMMUNICATIONS
LTD.**
2605 Alma St.
Vancouver, BC, V6R 3S1
(604)224-2384 **(PP)**

FAMOUS EVENTS LTD.
504 68 Waters St.
Vancouver, BC, V6B 1A4
(604)689-3448 **(PP)**

JACKSON PROMOTIONS
1321 Richards St.
Vancouver, BC, V6B 3G7
(604)683-8563 **(PP)**

THE LAZY GOURMET
2380 West Fourth Ave.
Vancouver, BC, V6K 1P1
(604)734-2507 **(C)**

OUT TO LUNCH
563 West Broadway
Vancouver, BC, V5Z 1E7
(604)876-2830 **(C)**

REGENCY CATERERS
1017 West King Edward Ave.
Vancouver, BC, V6H 1Z3
(604)731-8141 **(C)**

Florists

**COUNTRY GARDEN
FLOWER MARKET**
2112 West 41st Ave.
Vancouver, BC, V6M 1Z1
(604)263-2121

THE FLOWER SHOW
4430 West 10th Ave.
Vancouver, BC,
(604)224-3711

**THOMAS HOBBS
FLORIST LTD.**
2127 West 41st Ave.
Vancouver, BC,
(604)263-2601

Party Spaces

**BC ENTERPRISE
CENTER**
Indoor/outdoor areas on
    Expo 86 site
(604)682-2311

**CECIL GREEN PARK
HOUSE**
1912 home on a cliff
    overlooking water
(604)228-6289

**ROBSON SQUARE
MEDIA CENTER**
Part of courthouse and art
    gallery complex in city center
(604)660-2830

**VANCOUVER TRADE AND
CONVENTION CENTER**
City landmark under huge
    white sails on the harbor
(604)641-1410

Index